To Howard –

Praise for A Different Kind of Courage

Don't read this if you are too ashamed to cry. But if you feel the need for unvarnished truth and a hunger for unconditional love, *A Different Kind of Courage* will bring a greater reality into your life.

Bob Seiple
Former President, World Vision, Inc.

"*A Different Kind of Courage* is a must read. Jim Horsley's story is a powerful, wonderful, emotional roller coaster that took me down in tears and raised me up in joy. Once I started reading, I couldn't put it down."

Norm Evans
NFL (retired) member of two-time
Super Bowl Champion Miami Dolphins
President, Pro Athletes Outreach

"Jim Horsley's life takes off from a small town in Idaho and charts a course to heaven. This book puts flesh and blood, heart and soul into the man behind the stick. In a world made bad by a hell-bound fallen angel, it's great to hear about a world made *better* by a heaven-bound Blue Angel."

Bob Shank
President, Priority Living

"Talk about leadership usually focuses on the leader's public persona and activities. But we desperately need those who can 'lead from within'—who have courageously faced the darkness of life and come through deeper and stronger. Jim Horsley's inspiring story is that of a man who has found the deep inner life which makes his outer life truly authentic."

Leighton Ford
President, Leighton Ford Ministries

"We found Jim's book both a pleasure to read and profitable! His insights touched us at several levels. As a pastor who also is a pilot, Louis was captured by the drama, adventure, and courage of this 'type A' male. As a woman and a parent, Colleen found the story of Jim and Sonya's marriage relationship and their connection with their children hopeful and inspiring."

Dr. Louis and Colleen Townsend Evans

A
Different Kind
of Courage

Jim Horsley
with Mark Cutshall

WORD PUBLISHING
Nashville · London · Vancouver · Melbourne

A Different Kind of Courage
by Jim Horsley with Mark Cutshall

Copyright © 1998 by Jim Horsley. All rights reserved.

Unless otherwise indicated, Scripture quotations used in this book are
from the Holy Bible, New International Version (NIV).
Copyright © 1973, 1978, 1984, International Bible Society.
Used by permission of Zondervan Bible Publishers.

Book design by Mark McGarry
Set in Minion

Library of Congress Cataloging-in-Publication Data
Horsley, Jim, 1946–
A different kind of courage / Jim Horsley with Mark Cutshall.
p. cm.
ISBN 0-8499-4015-X (hardcover)
1. Horsley, Jim, 1947– . 2. United States. Naval Flight
Demonstration Squadron—Biography. 3. Air pilots, Military—United
States—Biography. I. Cutshall, Mark. II. Title.
V63.H67A3   1998   98–17421
359.9'4'092—dc21   CIP

Printed in the United States of America.
9 0 1 2 3 4 5 9 BVG 9 8 7 6 5 4 3

Contents

CONTENTS

Acknowledgments

My interest in attempting *A Different Kind of Courage* would likely not have gone much further than a few good intentions and a stack of random thoughts, notes, and scribbled Post-its without the support and assistance of so many. Thanks to Steve Tucker, who coordinated an introduction to my agent, Sealy Yates, and to Tom Thompson and Sealy, who have believed in the project from the beginning and offered their confidence and direction in guiding it to completion. Mark Cutshall has provided so much more than I could have ever hoped as my co-author; he has become an enthusiastic partner, dear friend, and kindred spirit.

I'm grateful for the cooperation, prayers, and support from Don and Molly Mowat, Phil Smart Sr., Shirley Lansing, Dave Baker, Max Carey, Russ Donnicci, Dave Dornsife, Bart Hansen, Hank Raehn, Steve Ridgway, Mike Nord, Bruce Davey, Rev. Ben Cross, Judie Belka, Tonya Clark and her son Tad, and my new friends at Word Publishing.

Mom and Dad have each provided keen perspective and loving support throughout this project, and I'm deeply grateful for them, and for their love.

A Different Kind of Courage could not have happened without the commitment, strength, and sensitivity of my wife, Sonya, and my children Jeff and Shannon's ideas, insights, and honest critique. I have been blessed beyond measure by their love and encouragement—this book is dedicated to them.

Introduction

On a steamy, sun-baked summer morning, we taxied into position on the runway for our four-plane Diamond Takeoff High-Performance Climb. It was Wednesday, a practice day for the Blue Angels. I was strapped in and ready to go. Using the plane's intercom, I checked with my passenger in the back seat of our narrator's two-seat TA-4J Skyhawk to ensure he was cinched down and ready to go. Sweat dripped down his face as he replied, "All set, Jim." Rear Admiral McDonald, the Naval Flight Demonstration Team's top boss, wanted a firsthand look at what the air show looked like from a pilot's perspective, and I was going to provide it for him.

Our flight leader called, "Run 'em up. . . . Power is set." I shoved the throttles forward to 85 percent rpm. My feet strained against the brake pedals. Each pilot rapidly checked his engine instruments and passed a thumbs-up to the "Boss" in Blue Angel number one.

"Off brakes . . . *now.*"

At the call "Adding power," we rapidly accelerated down the runway and lifted off, and I swiftly slid just under plane number two and up into the "slot" position behind and below the Boss's tailpipe.

Our Diamond formation thundered into the haze. The landing gear came up, the smoke came on, and we were into the practice show. I was too occupied to get into a prolonged conversation with Admiral McDonald, but he grunted an occasional "Okay" as I talked him through everything we were doing in the formation. Three maneuvers later, the Boss called, "Up . . . we go," and in unison, our four jets commenced a smooth climb leading into the Diamond Roll. At the "O . . . kay," we began a slow roll to the left, locked in our formation—thirty-six inches from wingtip to canopy and flying at a speed of nearly three hundred miles per hour.

On the backside of the roll, the admiral couldn't help himself.

The two wingmen's wingtips locked in position dancing softly only three feet from my helmet. "Unbelieeeeeevable," he screeched through my headset, his inarticulate attempt to describe the indescribable. He had flown hundreds of combat missions and over a thousand carrier landings in about every jet the Navy had ever built. Yet what he was seeing, in one of our easier Diamond formation maneuvers, was so far beyond what he had experienced in all his years of aviation that it left him all but speechless.

That year, my second on the team, we flew nearly eighty air shows, performing in front of nearly five million people. With my five other teammates, I did things in and out of airplanes that defied gravity and reason. I basked in the applause and stature of being among the "best of the best."

And though I reveled in the adulation, toward the end of my tour, life on the inside was becoming frayed and fragile. I couldn't define it at the time, but the signs of a greater reality were unmistakable.

This book is the story of my unexpected journey. Of how I fulfilled my dreams as a young man and then learned they weren't enough. I had nearly lost all that truly counted—my marriage, my identity, and my direction. And yet, the best that life had to offer still lay ahead.

This is the story, the adventure, of how I was drawn to a place I had never been—and what it took to get there. Of how I stepped beyond my resume and comfort zone, and discovered all I ever really needed.

By finding a different kind of courage.

1

Finding a Dream

God Almighty hates a quitter.

—SAMUEL FESSENDEN[1]

T he moment it rolled into view, I knew what I wanted to do
with my life.

On that late Saturday afternoon, several other Navy midshipmen and I stood on the edge of the tarmac at the Corpus
Christi Naval Air Station on the Texas Gulf Coast. I had just completed my sophomore year on a Navy ROTC scholarship at
Oregon State University and was now into the second week of a
summer orientation program.

My life had become a nonstop, seventeen-hour treadmill of
physical exercise, classroom lectures, and precision drills. And I
loved it all—the rigor of obstacle courses, the late night studying,
the chance to thrive under pressure and survive even the bad
breath of a superior officer barking orders in my face.

With our two-hour fitness training complete, our group had
been given orders to relax and take the rest of the weekend off.
This meant taking a twenty-minute bus ride into Corpus Christi.

The temperature had climbed to 105 degrees, and I had begun to stick to the inside of my starched white uniform. We hadn't walked more than fifty yards from our barracks, when one of the guys stopped at the flight line.

"Just a minute," he said. "Let's check out this airplane." I turned my head in the direction of a high-pitched engine, and there it was, the jet I had seen only in training manuals.

The A-5 Vigilante jet was seventy-four feet long. It had been built by North American Rockwell and was designed, originally, to carry nuclear weapons. Everything about the A-5 radiated sleekness, strength, and power. Capable of doing more than twice the speed of sound, it was the largest jet airplane to fly off a naval aircraft carrier. And as it crawled by in front of me, I could count the rivets on the fuselage.

I had completely forgotten about a bus ride into Corpus Christi. The ground crew put the chocks next to the tires to ensure the jet's complete stop. The two engines wound down, and the canopies came open. The pilot lifted himself out of the cockpit, while someone steadied a ladder next to the plane. Then, this chiseled figure wearing a helmet, an oxygen mask, and a dark green G suit, who looked like he had just come from the far side of the moon, stepped methodically down the rungs. He had the torso of Hercules and walked around the airplane with a certain swagger. The plane's navigator followed in his footsteps. In that moment, everything I had ever wanted to do in life came into focus.

I wanted to be that pilot. I wanted to fly. It was as real as the smell of jet fuel, or the sun's glare on the A-5's metal skin, and I decided I would do everything in my power to make it come true. I had no idea what it would take to get there. If it was anything like my years growing up, I knew I would be in for a ride.

Crackling cold and bubbling out of the earth

A walking tour of Soda Springs, Idaho, my childhood home, would take about fifteen minutes, give or take two hundred years. Years after the exploration team of Lewis and Clark and thousands of settlers heading west on the Oregon Trail left their footprints on the ground, my grandfather's grandfather settled the southeastern Idaho town. Jagged peaks and lakes were abundant. Two miles east of town, near a rock enclosure, a stream of crystal-clear water bubbled out of the earth, and whenever I passed by it on my bike, I couldn't resist bending down and feeling the startling cold result against my cheeks.

Certain man-made wonders proved irresistible. There was the city park, where I played baseball day after day, and the Idan-Ha Theater, where I was sure metal robots from Mars were going to invade our country and take over Soda Springs before I could make it back home. I stuck my nose in places I never knew existed, and sometimes I wound up in places I never wanted to leave. My most vivid memory is of the old high school gymnasium where my dad often refereed basketball games. One cold, winter night, we bundled into his pickup truck and drove off into the dark until we pulled up in the parking lot of the gym. The next thing I remember I was standing in the doorway of a room filled with the screeching sounds of tennis shoes and the sweat of two tired teams.

If I stand in that doorway long enough, I can think back to another night when the stands were full and the gym was dark. At halftime, just before the players ran back onto the court, the lights came on, and six-year-old Jimmy Horsley was standing behind the wood backboard, where the adults had perched me on top of a wobbly stepladder. One of the players below threw me the ball, and I dropped it through the hoop.

I was too young and full of curiosity to pay much attention to life's boundaries—until the day I almost learned too late. When Billy Dubin and I walked home from fishing one day and saw a delapidated chain-link fence surrounding a sawmill logging pond, we thought the same thing: Fences are made to climb. All it took was a few good toeholds, a grip on the top rail, and a big leap, and we were standing next to a sea of floating logs. They had dried in the sun and would be easy to grab—or walk on. Billy crawled out onto one, and I imitated his technique on my own log. Hand first, then knee. Knees, then feet.

We hit the water at the same time.

As I looked down at the gray-green water, I heard Billy scream. His log spun like a greased rolling pin. And then I went under. The coldness stunned me. I bobbed back up and reached for the log. Its slimy, algae-covered bark defied my grip. I slapped at the slick, black underbelly, but the log just laughed and rolled away.

Because the art of swimming had never surfaced in the Horsley family gene pool, I flailed helplessly. I went under, again, and came up coughing. I reached for another black log, but it too spun away. After a few desperate lunges, I kicked my way to the edge of the pond where I could finally stand up. Billy coughed, and hacked, and spit his way to shore.

My lungs heaved, and my body shivered. I could wring out my clothes but not my fear. Until that day it never really occurred to me that I could die. And be afraid. I wasn't thinking about Billy but only the trouble that awaited me back home. Yet, through some divine mercy, disguised as pure, childhood luck, my mother never saw me come home and dash into my bedroom, where I peeled off my clothes, jumped naked in bed, and shivered uncontrollably at the thought that I had almost drowned.

Risk just seemed to run in my veins. A few years earlier, my younger sister, Nancy, and I had been sitting on the living room floor. I don't know which of us found the cigarette lighter, or who forgot the standing house rule: "Don't touch it."

The curtains were the first to go. I ran down the hall, crawled up on my parents' bed, and once under the covers, sounded the alarm: "Nancy started a fire in the fireplace! Nancy started a fire!"

When the smoke reached the doorway, it suddenly occurred to Mom we had no wood in the fireplace, and she bolted for the door. Dad smelled trouble and passed her in the hallway.

I stayed in the back bedroom until I heard the sirens, and when the fire truck pulled up, there were men and hoses everywhere. They kept the blaze contained to a blackened hole the size of a barbecue pit in the middle of the living room, through which our charred furniture had fallen into the basement. As the firemen paraded through the house, my Uncle Bill, who lived up the road, came over to me and put his long arm around my shoulder. He knew all hell was going to break loose once the fire truck left.

My dad's response didn't resemble a prayer. Even in the best settings, his mood could turn dark like the soot he brought home from his work at the nearby chemical plant. In time, I realized that he endured some of the worst imaginable weather just to earn enough money to house, feed, and clothe all of us.

His long hours meant our family vacations were few. In fact, I only recall one—a long drive to West Yellowstone National Park, where Dad sat me on the back of a bear. Even though the animal had big teeth, a huge mouth, and stood on all fours, I wasn't scared because I remember Dad easing me down onto the animal's back saying, "It's okay, Jimmy. I'm right here."

Like any young boy, I wanted that kind of assurance from Dad. I would look forward to traditional family gatherings, like Sunday mornings when we watched the weekly pro football game on television. It was just him, and me, and the Baltimore Colts, and I loved it.

Though I looked up to him, Dad could be a little unpredictable. One Christmas Eve, he walked in the house with his arms around a huge tree. The trunk, alone, must have been eight inches thick. I waited for Dad to build a stand out of two-by-fours. After leaning the tree against the living room wall, he disappeared, only to return with a hammer and four railroad spikes. Then, very methodically, he drove each spike through the base of the tree and into our living room floor. The tree never tipped over, but Mom almost fainted.

For awhile, as a young boy, I learned to count on certain things: baseball in the spring, the sulfur smell of spring-fed water, and December snow. But even these changed.

One more new mailbox

"Get your coat, Jimmy. We'll be leaving soon."

My mom's announcement at the breakfast table one May morning was all the forewarning I had that our family was moving from Soda Springs. I couldn't figure out why all of my belongings had already been packed in cardboard boxes, why we couldn't just drive by Billy Dubin's house on the way out of town, or how long we would be in the car.

Somewhere on the trip Dad said something about Phoenix, Arizona, where warmer days promised to bring him new work. At eleven, I didn't know what it meant to say "good-bye" to the only home I had ever known. I was just happy to sit up in the front seat of Dad's pickup with my German Shephard dog, Rusty.

We had been riding for twelve hours when we reached the Arizona desert just as the moon started to rise. Somewhere near Flagstaff, he parked the truck and stepped outside to stretch. Rusty joined him. After Dad smoked his cigarette, he announced it was time to leave.

I yelled for my dog, but he didn't respond. I called for him, first with my hands cupped to my mouth then with my fists clenched.

The only sounds I heard were an occasional passing car, and two million crickets.

Dad paced around until he was out of cigarettes, and I became nervous thinking he was about ready to give up and wouldn't wait for Rusty. Minutes passed until my head sank into my arms. Then, while I sat with my back to the truck's front bumper, out of nowhere, Rusty came running toward me. He licked my face and gave no explanation. Neither did Dad, as he ordered us back in the truck then stomped on the gas pedal.

I gravitated toward adventure. One evening, somewhere between dinner and going to bed, Dad asked me if I wanted to ride with him in an airplane to Soda Springs. I couldn't wait. The next week we climbed into a plane with a single propeller that was barely big enough for three people.

Who the pilot was, or why my dad needed to make the trip, I can't remember. What I saw outside my window I'll never forget. It seemed almost magical, to rise above streets, trees, and people where everything seemed in perfect order, and where green and brown fields rolled on forever. Though the flight lasted eight hours, it ended too soon. When we had to land, I wanted to do it all over again. I had seen a bigger, wider world than I ever imagined. That new perspective disappeared as soon as Dad and I got back to Phoenix and a living room littered with cardboard boxes waiting to be packed.

This time the new address was Layton, Utah, an Air Force town that stood in the shadows of the Wasatch Mountains thirty miles north of Salt Lake City. It would be years later before I learned that Dad, while working hard in Phoenix, hadn't been able to collect on payments from his remodeling customers. The move meant he could start over by going into the lumberyard business with his dad. For me, it meant more confusion.

A great loss, a greater lesson

It happened one afternoon after I came home from school. I stopped near the back door and waited for Rusty. He was gone. I called for him. "Rusty! Ruuuusty!"

Nothing.

I opened the screen door and saw Mom standing at the sink.

"Where's Rusty?" I asked. She looked out the window, wiped her hands on her apron, and turned to me.

"Something happened, Jimmy. A situation came up with Rusty."

She paused, and I swallowed.

"We had to give Rusty a new home."

"Why? Where? Who decided this?"

The shock and the questions ran together.

My mother gave no explanation. There was just a silent, awkward look and something about him now belonging to another family. I didn't stay to hear the ending. I slammed my fist against my bedroom door, buried my face in my pillow, and cried. How could this happen? How could something I cared about so much be taken away from me?

Betrayal. Rage. Mistrust. Loss. Feelings which I still didn't have words for exploded inside all at once. I was in the sixth grade, at a new school with kids I didn't know. I was growing like a weed, aware that something was happening to my body. I wasn't even sure how I was supposed to act.

When Rusty left, the only other thing I could count on was packing up and going somewhere new. That summer, after residing only a few months in Logan, our family moved five miles south to the neighboring town of Kaysville, Utah. Though the town's main industry was boredom, I always found something to do. Clover Club Foods had a plant next to the highway that ran through Kaysville. One Halloween night, a couple of friends and I noticed a large stockpile of cardboard boxes used to ship the company's potato chips. Working quickly in the back of the building, we collapsed them all. Then, while the nearest headlights were still two pin points on the horizon, we hauled the boxes into the middle of the road, lit them on fire, and ran. Laying flat on our bellies hidden by weeds in the nearby field, we looked up at the huge flames and the flashing lights of Kaysville's one, mighty fire truck. No one was hurt, and no one ever found out.

In Kaysville, I buried myself in sports. Because I could throw a tight spiral, I played quarterback in junior high. I felt just as comfortable playing basketball. At five feet nine inches and 120 pounds, I was a natural eighth-grade power forward. What I lacked in muscle I made up for in passion.

In Kaysville, high school basketball wasn't played, it was worshiped. The congregation gathered in the Davis High School gymnasium. The pep bands and crowds brought a ritual of organized chaos to Friday nights. The man responsible for this was Grant Cullimore, whose team the previous year had won the state championship in Ogden. I had witnessed the game inside a field house that roared. With their title, Cullimore's players took on mythical proportions. Their stature among townsfolk rose with each week, fueled by newspaper articles and fresh heapings of public adulation.

I was one of the worshipers, in awe of the team and its coach. Aside from the fact I knew his daughter from school, I was sure Coach Cullimore had little idea of who I was as a wiry little guard, averaging eight points on a losing team.

That all changed one day in April when I heard the doorbell ring. I opened the front door and there, looming larger than I had ever seen him stand with his team on the court, was Coach Cullimore. Though big and wide, he carried no extra weight. He simply looked at me and said, "Hi, Jim." His calm, yet serious, voice said to me, "Pay attention because something important is about to happen."

Was I dreaming? The legend had come to my house *to see me*.

He handed me a box and told me to open it. I lifted the lid. Inside was a new pair of white high-top tennis shoes. "You need to break these in," he said. "We've got some plans for you."

I couldn't talk. I had never had a conversation with Coach Cullimore, and I wasn't sure I was going to break the string. To think that he was considering me to be part of a team he coached was almost overpowering. His visit to my house, his gift and endorsement of who I was, made all of the moves, the miles, and the strange new schools worth it.

It took several days to let Coach Cullimore's offer sink in—and just one piece of news to crush it. A few weeks later, because of Dad's ever changing job, we moved to Logan, Utah. Though I wasn't taking notes on my life, I must have logged an emotional entry that said, "One more new place. One more time to start over. No time to make memories, only time to pack boxes, unplug the refrigerator, and load the couch into the truck."

I didn't allow myself to feel anything. I just went along, and the good times followed. I entered high school and learned to drive. I took mandatory ROTC, wore the uniform, and liked it. I met Ann Bergner, who had a marvelous smile and said yes the first time I asked her out. And while Logan wasn't in the same league as Davis High School, I still gravitated toward sports, whether it was in a packed gym or on a football field under the lights.

The landscape changed one more time, when we moved to Billings, Montana, on a black night that was so windy the snow never touched the ground. At Billings West High School, the guys buttoned their shirts to the top button, and everyone seemed to have identical crew cuts. At the year's first assembly, I sat on a bleacher seat and stared straight ahead, wondering what on earth I had in common with these strange-looking kids. In a school that had just won the state high school basketball championship, I was an instant outsider. Acceptance came as I began throwing the football. As a junior, I was named honorable mention all-state at quarterback. At 135 pounds, I was probably the skinniest person to ever hold that honor.

Whatever the season or the contest, whenever I played, I wanted to win. Period. I spent hours shooting free throws, throwing passes, and studying play books. I wanted to be as good as I possibly could. Yet the real reason I worked so hard is that I didn't want to fail. One afternoon, a man put my resolve to the test and taught me an object lesson I still carry with me.

His name was Bob Greaves, and he was the head track coach who guided me along as a half miler. Four days before an important meet, he gathered all of the runners at the starting line on the track and said, "I want all of you to run a timed quarter mile." All of us looked surprised. Running one lap wasn't the long-distance or interval training we were used to.

Coach Greaves blew the whistle and off we went. I pushed out hard and still saved enough for the final turn. As we came across the finish line, he yelled, "Don't stop! Don't stop! Go another lap!" Under our breath, we swore. I sucked it up and kept going. I tried to maintain my stride, my form. At the 660-yard mark, I could see Coach Greaves walking across the field to meet us.

"Keep going! Keep going!" he yelled.

The pack had thinned out, most straining, and all wishing for this cruel practical joke to end. I came down the straightaway, completing 880 yards, twice the distance I expected to run. Again, Greaves walked back across the field. Certainly he would tell us to stop.

"Keep going! I want all of you to keep going!" I ran another hundred yards. As I started around the far turn, I staggered off the track, one of the last to die. Guys were coughing, writhing, and holding their sides.

When we regained consciousness, we sat on the grass, and Greaves asked, "How did it feel? When did you decide to quit?"

We were unanimous. "By the end of the first lap, the length you said we had to run," said a teammate.

"How unhappy were you with me when I told you to keep going?" In the most sensitive way possible, one of the guys said, "We wanted to kill you."

"Here's the point, gentlemen. What you have just learned is that your mind will always quit before your body will."

I thought back to how I felt at the end of one lap. I had wanted to quit. But Greaves had said, "Keep going." Every time my mind said, "Give up," he said, "Keep going," until I had run twice as far as I had expected.

Bob Greaves prepared me well. That spring, as a junior, my half mile times earned me a spot at a divisional meet in Great Falls, not just in my chosen event but in the mile—a distance I had never trained for, *a distance twice as far as I had ever thought I could run.* The kicker was that I had to run the mile less than an hour after I had put everything I had into the half mile. That day, running against the best milers in the eastern part of the state, I finished third, because I wouldn't quit.

For some reason, I listened

At the time, it seemed like a coincidence, but it changed my future forever. In my senior year of high school, a high school counselor, who saw I might have some leadership skills, suggested I apply for a scholarship in the Navy's ROTC program. Though I had been eyeing a possible track scholarship from the University of Utah, for some reason, I listened. I liked the idea of free tuition and books, and the required organization and discipline. Once accepted, the choice between the University of Colorado, the University of Utah, and Oregon State University was simple. Oregon State had just gone to the Rose Bowl the previous year. If that wasn't enough, my grandfather, whom I had respected tremendously, had played football for OSU in 1919.

That fall, I began living a regimen of early-morning wake-ups and close-order drills. The thought of naval aviation never occurred to me until my second summer orientation when I found myself on the tarmac in Corpus Christi looking up at a jet and the pilot who climbed out.

That afternoon something clicked.

All of my attention, my appetite for adventure, my desire to not fail, and my will to keep trying and hoping—whether it was a boy calling out for my dog or a high school quarterback calling the plays—all I really knew about myself and what I was cut out to do surfaced that afternoon.

By way of Soda Springs, Bob Greaves, and all the addresses in between, I had finally found my dream.

2

How Fast Could I Climb?

The aeroplane has unveiled for us the true face of the earth.

—Antonie de Saint-Exupéry[1]

The engine howl of the A-5 Vigilante and the helmeted pilots who emerged from its cockpit preoccupied my senses for days. I can laugh, now, yet at the time I never thought that pursuing my dream would leave me feeling so exhilarated and numb. In four brief, tumultuous years, I went from being a sunny university student who couldn't point out the pitot tube on a single-engine Piper Colt to a supremely self-confident aviator in the upper echelon of the Navy's carrier aviation attack pilots flying the A-6 Intruder. Getting there was a long, steep, grinding climb.

Down the runway

During that summer in Corpus Christi, the Navy wanted to get every midshipman up in an airplane to see how he would respond in flight. Would he panic? Would he adapt? These and other unspoken questions filled the air at an early-morning briefing on the eve of my first flight in a Navy aircraft. I sat in the ready room of the World War II vintage aircraft hangar with fifty other "middies" as a team of flight instructors fired a stream of figures and facts that could have filled a small almanac about the thirty-minute flight each of us was about to take.

"Any questions?" the leader asked. When no one responded, we filed out to the flight line where dozens of orange T-34 single-prop trainers were parked. If the A-5's pilot and navigator looked superhuman, then I must have looked like Forest Gump. Nothing seemed to fit. The helmet had wires hanging out everywhere. The visor seemed twisted. And the torso harness felt like a bad invention.

In the hundred-degree heat, I could feel my anxiety rise as I shook hands with the flight instructor. He wore a no-nonsense stare and seemed nonchalant. After all, he would probably repeat this flight four hundred times during the summer, including six or seven other times this day.

"It doesn't look like much, but you'll have your hands full," he said, motioning me to the plane.

"Yes, sir," I said, trying to project a feeling of confidence and understanding. In reality, I knew little about the flight. Even though I had been briefed on every switch and instrument setting, I was too focused on being airborne, too uncomfortable, too eager, to really listen. Yet, I wrote down all of the specifics of the pending flight on a five-by-seven-inch kneeboard card. This was affixed to a metal plate strapped to my right knee, so that if I needed to know an important radio frequency, navigation checkpoint, or sequence of maneuvers, all I had to do was glance down.

I lowered myself into the cockpit directly behind the flight instructor. In front of me were a stick, a throttle, and a black instrument panel filled with a maze of unfamiliar dials and gauges. The crew chief helped strap me in, and for the next few

minutes I absorbed the methodical process of how a pilot pre-
pares a plane for flight.

"Circuit breakers in."

"Battery on."

"Starting the engine."

The instructor's words crackled in my ear as the engine
coughed, then roared to life. Once the canopy slid forward over
the cockpit and locked in place, the stream of pretaxi checks
became a real-time soundtrack to the parade of other T-34s
rolling by outside my window.

"How you doing, Jim?" he asked.

"Ready to go," I said, with all the bravado I could muster.

A crewman removed the chocks that held the T-34 Beachcraft
in place, and we taxied to the takeoff hold-short area. The pilot
then asked me to put my hand on the stick so I could follow him
through the controls and experience each of the delicate motions
required for takeoff.

We were now moments away. Before I could swallow, I heard
the tower chief in my ear. "Cleared for takeoff."

"Ready to go, Jim?"

"Yes, sir," I said.

The instructor released the brakes and went to full power.
Immediately the tiny T-34 seemed to leap down the runway. The
air speed indicator needle sprang to attention. Against a slight
crosswind, the flight instructor firmly coaxed the airplane on the
runway centerline straight ahead. Then at ninety knots per hour,
I felt the stick in my hand rotate back.

The rumble of the plane's wheels ceased, and up we went.
Gradually, all of the people and protocol of the morning faded
away.

We were airborne and rising at one thousand feet per minute. It
was so simple and seamless, without friction, like a kayak slicing a
path through still water. While the engine turned at twenty-five

hundred revolutions per minute, the cockpit remained strangely quiet, except for the instructor's communication with the tower. "Corpus Tower, Two Sierra, One One Seven airborne, departing to the south." My mind was a blur as I tried to keep up with the sequence of next steps.

"Okay, Jim, gear and flaps are up, engine instruments normal. We're headed one niner zero climbing to three thousand. Keep your head on a swivel for conflicting traffic."

I looked out at a denim blue sky. Our air speed indicator crept up to 160 knots, and we leveled off at three thousand feet.

"Jim, you ready to take the controls?" the flight instructor asked.

"You bet," I said, with no hesitation.

I looked straight ahead and could see him raise both hands. I now had control of the airplane. Gingerly, I tightened my grip.

What a marvelous feeling. For the first time, I was flying.

I moved the stick, first to the left, then to the right. Even with the slightest touch, the T-34 responded. All of the training manuals and classroom lectures now gave way to a new reality. Once airborne, I had to constantly think on three planes: lateral (side to side), horizontal (forward), and vertical (up and down). This new perspective would one day help decide my fate in far less friendly skies.

I had just begun to feel comfortable with the stick in my hand when the instructor said, "Okay, Jim, I've got it." I let go and instantly felt relieved. I had survived this first opportunity to pilot an airplane.

"Now, we're going to do a series of maneuvers." For the next several minutes, I began to learn what an airplane could do.

A series of bank turns revealed the correlation between angle of bank and the necessity to keep the nose level. The steeper the bank, the more the nose of the plane would tend to drop below the horizon. And that meant the pilot needed to feed in more back stick, thereby increasing the pull, or "g-loading," to maintain flight.

In our most impressive stall, the flight instructor pulled the stick sharply back with the engine at full power. For the airplane it was pure aggravation, like a dentist sticking a drill in one's mouth and refusing to back off, while the patient continued to squirm.

Descending in a fifteen-degree dive at full power from three thousand feet, we accelerated to 185 knots. Then, with the aircraft stable at fifteen hundred feet, the instructor pulled back smartly on the stick, and we entered the front half of a full, 360-degree loop. It felt like a lead weight had dropped onto my chest, as the three g's—or 510 pounds of pressure on my 170-pound body—pinned me deep into the seat. The instructor eased the stick back, while the plane floated inverted over the top of the loop and came down the backside. I would have thrown up, if I had known where "up" was.

After a few more loops, one of which I managed to perform, we climbed to six thousand feet. The instructor pulled the power to idle and continued to pull the stick back into his lap, as the plane decelerated. Then, he kicked in full left rudder, and the plane flopped on its back and headed straight down. We were vibrating like a jack-hammer when the instructor neutralized the rudder pedals, added a little power, and released back pressure on the stick and the aircraft quickly regained stabilized flight.

It was obvious the pilot knew precisely what to do. Nothing surprised him. He did exactly what he wanted. By using the right controls at the right time, the plane responded immediately. In fact, even when it was seemingly out of control, the Beachcraft responded to the pilot's touch and flew beautifully, exactly the way it was designed.

Something else amazed me. I didn't get sick, nor did I feel scared or nervous. In fact, even with all the strange-sounding aviation acronyms floating in my ears, I actually picked up a lot more of the in-flight commands than I thought I would. Several times, the flight instructor asked, "Does this make any sense to you?" and I said, "No problem. This is great. Let's try it again."

The next day we did, putting the T-34 through much more aggravated, prolonged spins of seven and eight revolutions. With every new maneuver and level of calculated risk, my respect for the airplane, and for the instructor, grew. And I realized how quickly I could get into trouble if I didn't pay attention and fly right. But it wasn't my time in the T-34 that convinced me I wanted to fly.

The Marines miss their target

After three weeks of flight orientation in Corpus Christi, the Navy flew our midshipman class to Camp Pendleton for two weeks prior to heading to San Diego and a couple of weeks at the Navy's Amphibious School. After that I would commit to serve in either the Navy or the Marine Corps upon my graduation from Oregon State.

The Camp Pendleton experience had all the appeal of a root canal. The Marines' idea of orientation was to throw us an M-1 rifle with blank ammunition, assign us to a platoon, then, while announcing which way was north, march us off into miles of scrub brush and dirt. It meant wearing camouflage and surviving on canned rations that, hopefully, didn't have anything swimming around in them. And that was just the warm-up.

After we awoke from our night exercises exhausted, hungry, and dirty, the officers took little notice and perched us on a hillside to witness an air-to-ground firepower demonstration. "Gentlemen, please direct your focus to the valley," barked the Marine major. "You'll notice several tanks. Those are the targets."

Moments later, two F-4 Phantom Navy jets roared into view. At 450 knots, vapor streaming off their wings, they thundered downward toward the ravine in front of us. First they swooped in, firing thirty-millimeter canons. On their second pass, they flew so close that even from a half mile away I could see the canisters underneath the planes' bellies tumble toward the tanks. I looked back at the departing Phantoms, their pilots doing victory rolls across the horizon, and said to myself, "That's you."

Three seconds of thunder

I must have done something right, because in the early spring of my junior year I was selected with one other NROTC classmate at Oregon State for the Navy's summer international excursion, a six-week cruise aboard the USS *Independence* in the Mediterranean. Our destination was Istanbul, Turkey, where we boarded the massive ship.

To say I was awestruck by the four-thousand-man crew and the flight deck and hangar bay filled with jets is an understatement. Being assigned to Fighter Squadron (VF) 41 meant rubbing shoulders with Navy pilots flying airplanes off the carrier. Then I discovered I would get a ride in a Navy F-4J Phantom.

The news was almost too much. Everything about the flight gear—the G suit, the torso harness, the helmet—fit so much better than it had on my maiden voyage in the T-34. By anyone's standards, the F-4J was an exceptional military aircraft. It could fly at a speed of mach 2.4 and carry an arsenal of Sparrow and Sidewinder air-to-air missiles, along with twelve five-hundred-pound bombs. Plus, it had set numerous time-to-climb records and was the backbone of the Navy's fighter capability in Vietnam.

Walking across the flight deck, I felt the scurry and hum of crews preparing airplanes to launch. Before I could size up the F-4's imposing bulk, I was easing myself into the cockpit, where the crew chief strapped me in the seat directly behind the pilot.

The F-4's two huge J79 General Electric engines rumbled to life, the clamshell canopies lowered into the closed position, and we taxied forward under the flight director's guidance. Then the plane's holdback cables were attached to the ship's catapult shuttle, and the pilot ushered me through a series of takeoff checks.

The flight deck catapult officer gave us the five-finger extension, rapidly opening and closing his hand. The pilot slammed the throttles into afterburner while the F-4 remained restrained on the flight deck, bright orange flames thundering from the exhaust cones. The airplane resembled a giant blowtorch.

The catapult officer touched the deck, and in less than three seconds, the aircraft rocketed from 0 to 175 knots. It was an unbelievable sensation, like someone had shot us out of a canon.

Almost as fast as the plane launched, the feeling of acceleration lessened, and a quietness came over the cockpit. With the streaking jet stabilized in a climbing attitude, the pilot retracted the landing gear and guided the F-4 upward.

I was stunned at how fast we climbed—two thousand feet in the first twenty seconds. On our way to six thousand feet in the first forty-five seconds. The airplane responded to the pilot's touch with smoothness and grace. In less than five minutes, we were at twenty-five thousand feet and thirty miles from the carrier. At thirty thousand feet, we had company. Another F-4, our wingman on the practice intercept flight, joined up, and together we made several sweeping reversals and turns.

From the first rivet up, the F-4 was designed to be nothing less than the most powerful fighter aircraft in the world. After a high-speed pass just eight hundred feet above the carrier deck, or accelerating vertically straight toward the heavens, I didn't need to be convinced. Upon landing, the arresting hook engaged the cross-deck cable, and we slammed to a sudden stop. I climbed out of the cockpit soaked in sweat.

For the next several days, flying was all I could think about. A few months earlier, I had become airborne in a little different way.

Maybe it was her smile

I don't remember the weather, or even who was ahead. But I remember her face, her impish grin, and most of all, her dimples. At my fraternity's volleyball game that summer evening, I learned her name was Sonya Lozier. And that she was ruthless.

"Don't hurt yourself," she teased as I dove at the net to return her slam.

It took me two weeks to finally get up the nerve to ask her out on a date. The day before the Big Event, a flag football game swept me off my feet. Running around left end, I stumbled and turned my left knee into a free-swiveling universal joint. With my one remaining good leg, I somehow guided a friend's '55 Chevy to within walking distance of the curb at Sonya's sorority house. Everything else that evening, and that semester, remains fuzzy, except for two significant mileposts:

After the twelfth date, I found the courage to kiss her.

In the spring of my junior year, we became engaged. The moment was burned in my memory because that summer, while I was at sea on the USS *Independence*, a letter arrived one day. Sonya's handwriting was unmistakable. So was her message:

"The engagement is off." Sonya had seen the signs of my impetuousness and immaturity, and the summer separation and anxiety of an uncertain future were more than she wanted to deal with.

The words went right to the heart. I knew it was over. That fall, less than two weeks after being back on campus, I ran into Sonya at the Beaver Hut, a favorite Corvallis watering hole. Slowly, somehow, we began to rebuild our relationship. Whatever future we had together, including the possibilities and fears of a continuing relationship, came down to a dinner over pizza.

I knew I loved her, but I wasn't sure I knew how to make it all work.

"I know that after graduation I'm headed to flight school, and I want you to go with me," I told her, unsure of exactly what I would say next. "If you don't go with me, I'll consider your decision final because I don't want to look back over my shoulder at a relationship with loose ends."

Ten days later on Halloween night, standing outside the apartment where her now-retired parents lived, I asked Sonya to marry me. Four days before Christmas, we walked down the aisle of the Episcopal Church in Corvallis, Oregon, unaware of a fractured Chinese proverb that forewarned, "The honeymoon journey of a thousand miles begins with a single, broken tire chain."

In our first seventy-two hours as newlyweds, we drove three hundred miles through snow, ice, and anxiety in a '65 Dodge Dart. One hundred miles from Shoshone, Idaho, our vows took on new meaning, when after chaining up and heading into a blizzard, something snapped.

Thwap! Thwap! Thwap! One of the tire chains had broken. I nursed the car to a stop in the swirling snow and got out. After finding nothing in the trunk, I asked Sonya if I could use one of her shoelaces. Sonya said yes, and I tied the knot—again.

A few miles down the road, I heard romance in the air. Ka-thwap! Ka-thwap! Ka-thwap! Same noise. Same chain. Same solution. Sonya's second shoelace lasted just five minutes. Grace finally prevailed when a passing farmer stopped to offer me a handful of bailing wire to rehook the chains. That night, Sonya and I praised his name all the way to our sub-tropical destination of Billings, Montana, where, after midnight, we froze to a stop.

When we finally thawed out that spring, Sonya and I had built the foundation for matrimonial harmony. We acquired our first dog, Gomer. We bought our first television from a local motel owner. From his other aging black-and-white sets I found a knob to actually turn on our "new" ten-dollar home entertainment treasure.

That April, I made a deal with Sonya: Any money I earned over forty hours per week would pay for flying lessons. The Piper Colt wouldn't beat the T-34 in a beauty contest, but it took me where I had always wanted to go. After three weeks of ground school and six flights with an instructor, I walked out onto the tarmac at Corvallis's Muni Field for my final exam.

The test began with some level turns and stalls, then several touch-and-go landings. The instructor directed me to roll to a stop on my third landing, then got out and said, "She's all yours, Jim." Three minutes later at the takeoff end of the runway, I gunned the Piper Colt and then, with wings rocking slightly, climbed into the air.

The exhilaration of flying with no one looking over my shoulder quickly faded when I had to get turned down wind, complete the landing checks, and begin my first approach.

After two touch-and-go landings, I touched down and taxied to a stop.

I had soloed. Though Oregon State University pinned no wings on me that June at graduation, I could feel the excitement building three thousand miles away.

Touching down—on the dining room table

The Navy's Flight Training Program in Pensacola, Florida, had been founded in the early years of military aviation for one purpose: to train a select group of qualified aviators for carrier operations. By the summer of 1969, nothing had changed. The war in Vietnam only increased the intensity level in our class of two hundred. History was not on our side. Half the classmates would wash out. At best, only 10 percent, around twenty individuals, would eventually qualify for assignment to jet aircraft. The remaining graduates would be left to fly straight-wing prop aircraft like the T-34 and other support and training planes. I knew which kind I wanted to fly, and it didn't come with a propeller.

Flight school began in Pensacola, Florida, a week after my June graduation. Within hours of arriving by car from Oregon, I was preyed upon by a mobile home dealer who made selling used cars seem like a called profession. With all the class of a polyester suit, he almost persuaded me to sign a deal that would have had Sonya and me paying on aluminum siding into retirement.

Fortunately, we settled on a small cinder block apartment outfitted with a red plastic couch and sandblasted linoleum. A few days later, I upgraded the decor and bought my wife a braided rug. A second "Great Moment in Rental Living" occurred when a door-to-door vacuum cleaner salesman offered us a free set of steak knives just for sitting through a brief, in-home demonstration. Hurricane Sonya struck minutes later when I accepted the steak knives and declared to her that we really didn't need the vacuum.

Still, we celebrated. Doug Connell and Hal Pike, two friends whom I had met during summer orientation, had also made it into flight school. The three of us organized a mini-reunion golf match that began at nine o'clock in the morning. After completing eighteen holes by four o'clock that afternoon, we took three hours to finish off the nineteenth hole. When Doug's bride, Cathy, finally tracked us down, she was less than amused, announcing that the roast beef she planned to serve for dinner was now the size of a charcoal briquette.

On the first day of flight school, I checked my ego at the door.

The regimen was nothing to blink at. After ground school from 7:30 to 9:30 A.M., we faced two hours on obstacle and cross-country courses before launching into five hours of classroom training and library study. Intense cramming was required. Sleep was an elective.

The "Dilbert Dunker" was not. This cockpit apparatus had been created to simulate emergency rescue in a water emergency. As soon as the nose sank into twelve feet of water, the student-pilot had less than twenty seconds to undo his seat harness and escape, or be pulled up from the water by scuba-equipped staff. It was either sink or swim, literally, because failing Dilbert meant you were out of flight school.

After conquering Dilbert, I had to jump into an eight-foot-deep pool, strip off the thirty pounds of flight gear, then swim a mile in my flight suit. Because I had taken a swimming course at Oregon State the previous year, my mile time allowed me to waive several grueling weeks in the pool and catch up on studying, and Cokes, at the library.

In flight school, every assignment called for sweat, smarts, or both. The Navy didn't reward attitude, only results. Even though I already had a single-engine pilot's license, the three to four weeks of ground school needed to fly the T-34 became nothing less than a simple, yet crucial, pass-fail exam. To help prepare me for the actual solo, Sonya read aloud the multitude of mandatory checkpoints, altitudes, voice calls, and engine instruments I committed to memory, as I "flew" the T-34 around the kitchen table.

My biggest obstacle, however, was in the air. His name was Captain Ross. This Marine officer who reviewed my check ride for the T-34 was one cheeseburger shy of 250 pounds. His military motto was "Better be dead than look bad," and he proved it one day by relishing his reputation as a "screamer." According to legend, Ross had become so incensed at one student pilot that the captain unfastened his metal kneeboard and threw it at the pilot's helmet. It bounced off the helmet and flew out the open canopy into space, notes and all. On my day of decision, Captain Ross calmly climbed aboard the T-34, okayed my touch-and-go-landings, and later okayed my solo. For some fortunate reason, I had failed to inspire a sequel.

...and flashes of blue

Being selected for jet training, after making the cut, ratcheted up the pressure. We packed our steak knives and fuzzy television set and moved to Meridian, Mississippi, where I had a date with a straight-wing, single-engine jet called the T-2 Buckeye. Ground school, procedures, and flight rules became more intense. From the flight simulators to my first time behind the stick, the pressure to learn increased exponentially.

Even the wives felt it. They were admonished by the commanding officer to "ensure the mental and physical preparedness of your husbands by fixing them a lumberjack breakfast of eggs, bacon, and toast." In our household, this lasted all of two days. I got sick of looking at scrambled eggs, and Sonya got sick of looking at me. In the interests of saving time, and my appetite, I switched to a typical fighter pilot's breakfast—a cup of coffee and a cigar.

In Meridian, I learned the meaning of "adrenaline rush." I felt it the day the Blue Angels flew into town for their famed air show demonstration. At the time, I was just beginning to grasp the concept of "formation flying," which, to young jet trainees, meant taking off on separate sides of the runway at five-second intervals. To the Blue Angels, who took off in front of me that Saturday, formation flying meant racing down the runway in a four-plane Diamond, with wingtips no more than three feet apart. The noise almost buckled my knees. For forty minutes it was nothing but thunder, and speed, and flashes of blue. I could barely comprehend what they did in the air, much less imagine myself ever being in their place. After six months in Mississippi I was back in Pensacola. Sonya was pregnant and headed home to see our families and escape the summer heat.

I needed to put my nose down and dive into six weeks of air-to-air gunnery and carrier qualifications. Hour after hour, I flew in formation, did touch-and-gos, and prepared to figure out how I would ever land a T-2 jet on an aircraft carrier. All I had to do was touch down on two hundred feet of floating runway at the exact angle that would allow the plane's tailhook to catch one of the four arresting cables that would bring me to a neck-snapping standstill in less than three seconds.

After ten flight hours, sixty-five practice carrier landings, and a zillion approach corrections at a nearby field, I finally got my chance in the Gulf of Mexico, where the USS *Lexington* cruised. As we circled overhead at ten thousand feet, the carrier looked no bigger than a postage stamp. Words like "impossible" began to stray into my mind's periphery. As I descended, the ship began to look like a high-rise office building floating on its side. I followed all the procedures and on my first attempt completed a picture-perfect touch-and-go. I got the command "Drop the hook" and completed four carrier landings and catapult launches with a feeling of accomplishment and satisfaction I'd never experienced. I celebrated with a cigar and saved the coffee for breakfast.

Days later, I arrived in Kingsville, Texas, for advanced jet training by way of Houston, where I rendezvoused with Sonya, in her seventh month of pregnancy. While she battled ninety-five degree humidity and Texas-sized gnats, I took the TA-4 jet through a ripsaw-like schedule of formation flying, air-to-air combat, air-to-ground bombing, air gunnery, and carrier qualifications.

When the dust finally settled, I had finished second in my class of fifty. I didn't pretend to think I knew more than others. I had simply worked hard to hone a few innate abilities like starting out prepared, not panicking in moments of high stress, and relying on the running map in my head that allowed me to comprehend my altitude, air speed, and fuel consumption all at once.

I marveled at guys who were naturally gifted in areas that didn't come quite as easily for me, like basic acrobatics. One classmate, who had flown as a crop duster, moved the stick with the grace and skill of a symphony conductor's baton. I, on the other hand, didn't immediately harmonize with the plane. I had to rely on practice and other resources like knowing how to anticipate and prepare. Flying the TA-4J at three hundred knots, I could consistently hit a series of navigational checkpoints while skimming over the terrain at altitudes of five hundred feet. In air combat training, I had an innate ability to anticipate the location of the other aircraft, and I always seemed to get my plane into the right position for various maneuvers.

Still, the pressure of flight school never let up. Only three out of ten trainees would get a jet seat, and only one in twenty (three in our class of sixty) would have the luxury of choosing which airplane he wanted to fly. Right in the midst of it all I could hear another high-pitched whine, not another jet but an impressive scream nonetheless. It was the cry of our first child, Jeff Warren Horsley: six pounds, seven ounces. Pink, loud, and beautiful.

The hospital loved me. Against orders, I took a flash picture of Jeff in the nursery and woke up the entire infant population. Yet, deep down, I was too preoccupied with flying to invest emotion or time with my newborn son. He was my joy, and an alarm clock that loved two o'clock in the morning. Waking up to Jeff's wailing early one morning, I saw and smelled the signs that Gomer, our dog, had plumbing problems as well. I trudged barefoot into the bathroom, where Sonya stood changing Jeff's diaper. Without thinking, I barked, "Can't you keep that baby quiet?" If Sonya didn't cry, she should have. I simply didn't have the tact or temperament for humane conversation. Flying three flights per day in hundred-degree temperatures and the heat of extreme competition had put me near the edge. I was too stressed to spell the word *compassion*, and too exhausted to care.

A few weeks later, on the morning of November 20, I got the news that I would graduate 2nd in my class of 100. The celebration didn't end until Sonya pinned the Navy's coveted Wings of Gold on my uniform in a ceremony at the base officer's club. And then I chose my airplane.

For years I had marveled at, studied, and flown the F-4. But, to me, it didn't have the allure of another airplane, one with a somewhat lesser reputation. It wasn't a high-altitude attack fighter but a low-level attack aircraft known for its bulbous nose and affectionate nickname, "the flying drumstick."

The plane was the A-6 Intruder. The first time I saw it up close and personal came days after flight school in January 1971, when I reported to the Whidbey Island Naval Air Station for A-6 training with the Attack Squadron VA-128. Merely learning about the A-6 was a load. The Naval Aviation Training and Flight Operating Procedures (NATOPS) manual was two inches thick. In its 250 pages was every procedure and requirement, warning, pre-flight check, performance chart, and operating envelope diagram needed for the pilot and bombardier/navigator to fly the twenty-eight-ton swept wing monster on tree-top level missions at 420 knots. Its side-by-side windshields looked like eyeballs on a fly. The A-6 didn't win me over with its good looks. However, American pilots returning from Vietnam revered its handling, compatability, and formidable payload of twenty-eight five-hundred-pound bombs. I had plenty to learn.

The ultimate test

After nearly one hundred flight hours in the A-6, I still needed my night carrier qualification. Bad weather and lack of sea time for the ship had thwarted my attempt a month earlier. The day after my twenty-fifth birthday, I launched from the Naval Air Station at Alameda and headed toward the USS *Hancock* steaming one hundred miles at sea off the coast of San Francisco. Orbiting thirty miles behind the ship at fifteen thousand feet, I tried everything I could to collect my wits for the ultimate test for naval aviators.

What seemed like an eternity in the air ended with the command "Cleared for your approach." Experienced pilots, flight manuals, and stories confirmed to me what I already knew: Landing a Navy jet on an aircraft carrier steaming ahead at twenty knots was a dicey task. Unlike civilian and other military pilots, only Naval aviators could put a "night trap" on their resumé, and I wanted to join the club.

My bombardier/navigator in the right seat informed the carrier of our progress as we passed through five thousand feet. Then, ten miles behind the ship, we stopped our initial descent at twelve hundred feet. To align my direction with the approach course to the carrier, I made a slight heading correction and began to slow the airplane to two hundred knots.

At six miles behind the ship, with the landing gear and hook down and the flaps extended, I checked my fuel weight and cockpit switches. Then I adjusted the throttles to stabilize the decelerating jet at 130 knots for the precise angle of attack needed for my final approach.

I knew the rule: Focus only on the landing area (called "meatball"), line up, and angle of attack. *Don't look at the ship.* Those pilots who peeked into the inky darkness were rewarded with the startling sight of a pitching deck, confusing silhouettes, and total disorientation.

Three miles behind the carrier and still level at twelve hundred feet, the ship's air controller said the words I wanted: "On course, approaching glide slope."

The speed brakes came out.

Descending at seven hundred feet per minute, everything looked good.

At less than four thousand feet behind the ship, the controller called, "November Juliet Eight Zero Five, three quarters of a mile, call the ball with your state." This was my cue to lift my scan from the instrument panel to look for the orange "meatball" on the carrier deck landing system frensel lens, or "mirror." From my cockpit, I would see it only if the plane was set at the proper attitude, glide path, and glide course—the precise window for an arrested landing.

I did exactly what I needed.

"Intruder ball, four point eight," I said.

"Roger, ball" replied the landing signal officer (LSO), who stood at the edge of the flight deck, adjacent to the mirror.

At that point I didn't remember anything I was supposed to be doing in the cockpit. The airplane's wings began to wiggle. I swiveled my gaze from the mirror and locked on the ship's masthead lights, a sure sign that I had gone from pilot to spectator of my own landing. I could still see the ball, but I hadn't made the proper power adjustments. All of a sudden, the LSO bellowed in my ear.

"Steady your wings, check your power!"

It was his last hope that I would realize my landing approach had deteriorated.

All this did was compound my confusion.

I was now one thousand feet from the ship.

Landing was no longer an option.

I completely forgot about landing the airplane.

I never touched the power. As the carrier's deck ballooned in size before my eyes, the LSO came up on the radio and said,

"Wave off! Wave off! Wave off!" I jammed the throttles forward and roared over the flight deck as the LSO came up again. "Eight Zero Five: The only way you'll get down flying like that is if we shoot you down."

I felt like my world had collapsed. No night carrier qualification. Not this time. I fought to make sense out of what had just taken place. Everything I had worked toward, all that I had dreamed about over the past two years, had suddenly disintegrated in less than thirty seconds.

Yet, somehow the months of training, study, and practice took hold inside me, and by the time I had climbed back up to twelve hundred feet and turned downwind for another attempt, I had regained a reasonable degree of composure.

The second attempt, a few minutes later, ended differently—in a calculated, successful landing, when the tailhook of the thundering A-6 snagged the number three wire. I secured my night qualification after duplicating the maneuver five more times. In the wee morning hours, relieved and almost out of gas, I flew back to the base. I had flown my way to the top. Yet, a new challenge awaited.

Within days I was assigned to VA-115, a fleet squadron that had just returned home from Vietnam with its cadre of veteran combat pilots. Though most of them were only a year or two older than me, they had a swagger and a seriousness about them that said, "I've seen the other side and returned. I've done the stuff you'll only dream of doing."

I had looked at a map of Southeast Asia, and while I didn't deny the reality of what lurked for me on the horizon, I wasn't ready for the news.

Four months later, on a sun-drenched Thursday afternoon, I landed my A-6 on the deck of the USS *Midway*, which had just arrived off the southern California coast from its home port in Alameda for two weeks of airwing exercises. But something wasn't right. Instead of directing me to taxi toward the catapult for my next launch, the flight deck personnel put chocks under my wheels and secured the aircraft to the deck with tie-down chains.

"Boss, do I have a problem?" I called on the radio.

"No," the voice said. "No one's going anywhere. We're headed back to port."

Immediately I shut down the plane's engines, got out, and walked to the ready room. There, on a large briefing board, were large black letters:

MONDAY MORNING, THIS SHIP SAILS FROM ALAMEDA
TO NORTH VIETNAM

At that moment, you could have knocked anyone on that ship over with a feather. Including me. In less than four days, two months earlier than I had planned, I was going off to war.

The next day, thanks to a Navy charter plane, the families of the various airwing pilots sailing with the *Midway* began arriving. One of those was a blonde twenty-four-year-old wife carrying an eighteen-month-old son who reached out and wanted to be held.

That Saturday night we dined one last time with Arlo Clark and his wife, Tonya. We were four bright young faces trying to believe in the future.

The future sailed away on Monday morning with wet eyes, and kisses, and a son who tried to open and close his hand, as if to say good-bye.

He was too young to understand. And I didn't have the words to tell him.

3

Welcome to the War

Some of the critics viewed Vietnam as a morality play in which the wicked must be punished before the final curtain and where any attempt to salvage self-respect from the outcome compounded the wrong. I viewed it as a genuine tragedy. No one had a monopoly on anguish.

—HENRY KISSINGER[1]

We had been warned.

On Monday morning April 10, 1972, the USS *Midway* steamed out of San Francisco Bay, bound for the Vietnam war zone. Everyone on board was aware that anti-war protesters would probably be standing on the Golden Gate Bridge, ready to pour gallons of blood-red paint on us as the ship passed under. But there was no rage blowing in the wind. As the carrier neared the mammoth suspension bridge, I looked up and saw a large American flag unfurled from the railings. While it rippled in the wind, a band near the passing cars overhead played a John Phillip Sousa march.

I grabbed my camera. "Mike, you and Gary look this way."

Neither Mike Penn nor Gary Shank (both A-7 pilots), nor myself, knew what was in store. Mike would spend seven months in a North Vietnam prisoner of war (POW) camp before being released. Gary would be killed in action. And I would come home, grateful to still be alive, yet not knowing I'd been wounded, although in a different way.

As the fog lifted that morning, a feeling of tremendous excitement and uncertainty filled the ship. But there was also a strange sense of eagerness on board. We were going off to fight in a war seventy-eight hundred miles away in a tiny Southeast Asian country. An isolated communist uprising in Vietnam had, over the course of ten years, hemorrhaged into a complex, costly military struggle involving hundreds of thousands of American combat troops. At least that many U.S. politicians, journalists, and college students, it seemed, had taken the offensive on different fronts. The debate raged on, from why it was wrong to get involved in the war, to what we needed to do to win, to how the United States had to get out.

For me, Vietnam began as a personal affair. As the San Francisco skyline receded to a memory, I kept smelling Sonya's perfume. I felt so empty and helpless leaving her standing there on the pier, especially since I knew she was two months pregnant. All I thought about was her, Jeff, and the baby, and how I would get through the next sixteen days en route to the Philippines.

The Navy had an answer. They filled every waking hour with meetings. Using chalkboards and endless lists, officers drilled and filled us with every conceivable procedure, from carrier operations and combat techniques, to what we could expect out of the airplanes. All of the details, orders, and bad coffee became a well-timed distraction.

Bob Ponton, my bombardier/navigator (B/N), and I had been flying together as a crew since our A-6 training on Whidbey Island. Now, working together, we had to plan for every contingency. His role in the cockpit was to operate the navigation, radar, and weapons systems. Mine was to ensure we had an equal number of takeoffs and landings. I had to get our jet in position to drop its weapons load and return safely from the target area. Bob was a skilled B/N, with a gentle demeanor but a bulldog resolve. I had great respect for his ability and character, and I couldn't have asked for a better partner in the air.

Once we pulled into the Navy's huge Subic Bay port facility in the Philippines, we were on North Vietnam's doorstep. This was our final rest stop, one last chance to stretch before launching into battle. Whether or not we admitted it out loud, all of us realized we were on the verge of something big. Three days later, reality dropped anchor.

Maiden voyage to An Loc

Our first air strike was a dot on the map called An Loc. This thatched-roof town had the misfortune of straddling the Ho Chi Minh Trail, the infamous supply route blazed by the North Vietnamese determined to capture South Vietnam's capital, Saigon. For months the North Vietnamese had been on the march, overrunning everything in their path. Because Saigon was essential to South Vietnam's survival, U.S. political and military leaders were determined to defend the city to the end, and that meant marshaling resources, including intensive air bombing, to spoil the enemy's plans.

On April 29, the day we launched to An Loc, the ship was steaming toward Vietnam, still some five hundred miles off the coast. We were so far out, in fact, that most of the launch aircraft required in-flight refueling just to make it to the target and back to the ship. The primary incentive, of course, was to fly successful missions. A "bonus" was the additional sixty-five dollars of combat pay everyone on the *Midway* received for each month in combat. Some bonus. We would find out soon enough that the extra pay would pencil out to about a buck-sixty per mission. How was I going to spend all that extra cash?

Our three A-6 attack-bombers, each loaded with twelve five-hundred-pound bombs, flew in loose formation as we headed inland. We were led by Commander Jack Presley, our squadron executive officer ("XO"), in the lead A-6. As we settled into a left-hand orbit overhead An Loc at eighteen thousand feet, Presley initiated radio contact with the Air Force forward air controller (FAC) circling the target area in an OV-10 Bronco. Just minutes prior to our intended target time, we were unexpectedly ordered out of the area by a radio command from the Air Force Command Center call on the standard emergency frequency that all aircraft monitored while airborne. "Arclight, arclight, arclight," with time and coded coordinates, indicated an imminent B-52 strike on the highway ten miles north of An Loc.

We rapidly shifted ten miles to the east of the reign of terror that fell from thirty thousand feet. Moments later we could see the shock waves rippling the jungle canopy on a line that seemed to stretch for several miles. The North Vietnamese troops would have no warning, and no escape. Seconds after hearing the whistling sound of bombs, they would perish in an oven of thunderous fire.

"A-6s holding high, descend to one zero thousand and report visual on me, over."

As we leveled off, the FAC's radio crackled. "Intruders, the area is hot with enemy presence in all sectors. Civilians have abandoned the area. Your target is two tanks parked right in the middle of town that's been vacated. Notify when visual on the target, over."

Each pilot rapidly scanned the maze of buildings and identi-

fied the tanks, calling, "Tally Ho, XO." The XO then made a similar call to the FAC, who immediately replied, "Give me four
bombs each on three passes, you're cleared in hot."

I adjusted my flight path to establish some separation from the
other two bombers. Seconds later, Presley's A-6 pitched slightly
nose high, then abruptly rolled 135 degrees to the left as he simultaneously called, "Leads in hot." Moments later, on a dive path
offset to his right, I replicated the same roll-in.

The war was on.

I rolled back to wings level at forty degrees nose down. With
my jet accelerating to 480 knots, two olive-green enemy tanks
snuggled against a large building filled up the bombsight
mounted on top of my instrument panel.

Everything I had trained for in Pensacola, Corpus Christi,
Meridian, and Whidbey Island coalesced in this one moment. As
Bob called out our altitudes at one-thousand-foot increments
during the dive, I adjusted the control stick. Then, as we passed
through forty-five hundred feet, without changing my grip, my
right thumb depressed the small red "pickle" button on top of
the stick grip. Four bombs rippled off the aircraft. Quickly, I
pulled the stick back in my lap to get the nose up and away from
the target area. Pressed back in my seat by the force of five g's, I
snapped the plane hard right to foil any anti-aircraft gunners
below.

"Great pass, great pass! Bombs on target!" the FAC called on
the radio. I was barely back on level flight path when the FAC
said, "Additional tanks are now moving down the street. See the
building with the thatched roof next to the palm trees?"

"Roger, that," I said. And down we went. Again.

Several hours after landing, I walked into the ship's ready
room and read the afternoon's results: "Flight of Intruders, lead
aircraft November Fox Five Zero Two on target at fourteen hundred. Three tanks destroyed, one damaged." Launch, strike, land,

and debrief. Then rest up for the next flight. I was ready to go out and earn another dollar and sixty cents.

Living at the speed of war

Two days later, we steamed into North Yankee Station, a staging area in the northernmost tip of the Gulf of Tonkin. If An Loc seemed like target practice, my first mission over "the north" put me right in the bull's-eye. We called them "armed reckys," short for "armed reconnaissance." In Vietnam, they were as common as shrapnel. The goal of two-plane armed recky strikes was to seek and destroy military ground "targets of opportunity." On my first armed recky, I wanted a guy with experience out in front. I must have been living well, because my assigned flight leader was just such a pilot. At twenty-six, Terry Young, or "Slick" as we called him, was a combat veteran, as was his B/N, John Bone, or "Bono." Tall and lanky, Slick always wore a mischievous grin that belied his savvy in the air.

We launched off the *Midway* on a gorgeous morning. A hundred miles from the coast of North Vietnam, our section of two A-6s descended in a spread formation, a tactical move to prevent an enemy gunner from hitting two planes at once with the same anti-aircraft artillery shells. Less than twenty miles from the beach line, we completed our combat checklist by arming our weapons panels and then streaked in over a beautiful crescent-shaped lagoon called Brandon Bay. As we approached the coastline at 420 knots, Slick and I began to weave (or "jink") left and right, up and down.

He was just three hundred feet ahead of me when disaster struck. As Slick maneuvered left to right and slightly below my flight path, I began a simultaneous roll in the opposite direction to the left. Suddenly, Slick's jet seemed to explode in a fireball.

His A-6 belched a huge cloud of white vapor and disappeared from sight.

I swung my plane around. All I could see on the ground was a plume of black smoke rising out of a riverbank. Bob shrieked, "They're down, they're down!" Immediately, I began climbing to get a safer, clearer view. There was no sign of Slick or Bono.

Bob switched radio frequencies. "Mayday! Mayday! Mayday! November Fox Five Zero Seven is down. Five Zero Two is in orbit. We need search-and-rescue support." Moments later, we were directed to clear the area.

Then, suddenly, Bob and I had another problem. Since we hadn't made our strike, we still were saddled with our twenty-two five-hundred-pound bombs, which made the A-6 as sluggish as a buffalo. We had only one option—to jettison the bombs at sea and, on the way back to the *Midway*, wonder about Terry Young.

As Bob switched to the carrier control frequency, I couldn't believe the voice in my ear.

"This is November Fox Five Zero Seven, inbound requesting ready deck on arrival."

It was Slick, still very much alive and sounding like his old self.

"Slick, call your posit," I demanded.

"I'm headed back to the ship like a scalded ape." Somehow, he had come through the fire. I called off the search-and-rescue crew. As the ship prepared for an emergency landing, I joined up with his plane and got close enough to assess the damages.

"Slick, you've got a hole the size of a basketball through your right wingtip," I radioed. I was stunned. The 37 mm gunfire had ignited only one fuel cell in the wing, but at least there had been no residual fire. With his new ventilation on display, Terry coaxed his plane onto the deck, where the gaping hole generated all the fervor of a flat tire.

"Hey, nice souvenir," said one of the flight crew. "You guys get some lunch. You're scheduled to fly in three hours."

Living at the speed of war, there wasn't time to rewind the

tape and comprehend why things happened. There wasn't time to wonder how, for instance, one bad outing could almost reduce a friend's resumé to an epitaph. An hour of personal reflection wasn't in the flight plan. I was moving too fast to let hindsight catch up and notify me that tomorrow's obituary could be Terry Young's. Or my own. On a pitch-black night a month later, I dealt with another casualty—the death of my invincibility.

Hold the doughnuts

We were on a single-plane strike locked on a group of supply vehicles rolling down the highway from China toward Hanoi. I stared intently at the luminous vertical display indicator on the instrument panel; it was all I needed to determine heading, altitude, and terrain clearance. I checked with Bob on the intercom. "Radar tickling us from one o'clock. How far from release?"

Suddenly, our instruments began twitching like a rattlesnake waking up from a nap. A North Vietnamese surface-to-air missile (SAM) search radar had us in its sights. Lights in front of me flashed: "MISSILE ALERT! MISSILE ALERT!" A high-pitched warning sound warbled in my ears. Then the entire instrument panel lit up like a Christmas tree. I could see the fiery exhaust plume of a SAM rising straight up in the distance ahead. I knew it was coming our way, because within five seconds it tipped over on its side. Instead of looking down at its plume, I saw a big, ugly "doughnut," the affectionate term for the flaming orange circle surrounding the dark hole in the middle. And it was racing right at us.

Jamming the throttles to full power, I rolled slightly left and pulled the nose of the A-6 down to pick up speed. We accelerated rapidly, and within seconds, I pulled back up into a fairly nose-high attitude to see if the missile was still tracking. It was. In my peripheral vision I saw a second missile erupt off its launch pad. I continued to pull the A-6 up. At nighttime, with no sense of distance, it was impossible to tell how near the missiles really were, or how fast a doughnut could fly at night.

Chaos reigned in the cockpit. Bob screamed in my ear, "Break left, break left!"

The warbling sound was now a pulsating, sick siren. The plane's radar warning scope flashed like a strobe light. Outside my window, I saw the orange glaze of a missile ready to eat me alive. I couldn't wait any longer. I snapped the A-6 to nearly inverted and thirty degrees nose down, and held my breath.

The first missile couldn't track with us and exploded as it passed behind. Down we plunged at 250 feet per second. Then, because the mountains hadn't changed elevation all evening, I had to pull up. We were just in time for the fireworks. Immediately off our left wing, the second missile exploded in a flash that lit up the entire sky. The A-6 shuddered from the concussion, as the missile's momentum propelled its lethal warhead past our left wing. To get out of harm's way, I leveled the wings and climbed to a safer altitude. Then I did something I had totally neglected in the rush to survive: I began to breathe again.

I had had a bucket full of close calls before, but until that night, I thought I was immune from injury, even death. Always, it had been "the other guy." From now on, however, I was on a first-name basis with fate. If I couldn't out-race my mortality in Vietnam, at least I could find a periodic time out.

Following each thirty- to forty-five-day combat period at sea, the *Midway* and its exhausted airwing and crew headed to port for some much needed rest and repairs. In Subic Bay, for instance, each squadron would send several of its aircraft ahead to the adjacent Cubi Point airfield for maintenance and aircrew proficiency training. Bored with the daily routine of poolside lounging, tennis, and too many dice games, three of us decided to take our A-6s for an early morning training flight to explore the surrounding countryside. Taking turns in a high-speed version of "follow the leader," we performed a variety of aerobatic maneuvers and roared through the spectacular valleys in low-level formation. Then it was my turn to take the lead.

To Bob's chagrin, I decided to see how low I could fly the A-6 before the radar altimeter quit reading. Thundering across the water one hundred yards off the beach-line, I coaxed the airplane lower and lower. I knew we were starting to skim the water when Bob quit breathing. Flying at 450 knots, ten feet below the altimeter limit of twenty feet, was about all my blood could stand. I pulled the nose up into a climb, and we created a rooster tail of magnificent proportions for the local residents. Playing this low-altitude version of chicken just a few feet off the water showed me how callous we had become to common sense. I would have felt worse if it hadn't been so much fun.

Running on empty

Leaving port always came too early. Back in the Gulf of Tonkin, we still had more work to do. Daylight multi-plane alpha strikes were as risky as single-plane night strikes and armed reconnaissance missions. Any of them could light the sky on fire and stop a pulse. By the end of my first month in the war, I knew the risks and rewards that awaited me every time I walked out on the flight deck. To survive, I had established my own standard operating procedure by acknowledging only one possible outcome—success.

I had it down to a routine. On my way to the plane, I always pulled the helmet-mounted sun visor down over my face. As a safety device, it protected my eyes from the sun's glare. And it provided a temporary shield against the outside world. With the visor down, no one could see in. No one could see my eyes, or read any of my facial features. No one could ever tell what I looked like, or who I was, much less what I was dealing with as I prepared to launch into the perilous encounters that produced the most unforgiving memories of the war.

The first came on a miserable, stormy day during an airborne refueling support mission. It wasn't my favorite type of flight. The tanker version of our A-6 was designed to "pass gas" to other aircraft, but we still needed to preserve two thousand pounds of fuel, six hundred of which were needed to get back to the ship and land and still have an emergency reserve of about fourteen hundred pounds. On that day, heavy seas, driving rain, and the *Midway*'s heaving flight deck were giving returning pilots fits. Only one of three was getting aboard on his first landing approach. One after the other, those who had "boltered" were popping up to an orbiting altitude of three thousand feet to take on enough fuel needed to attempt another landing.

As our fuel gauge dropped just below two thousand pounds, I radioed the ship that we were at minimum fuel and needed to commence our approach. The call came back: "Negative November Fox Five Two One, maintain altitude and pass one thousand pounds to the fighter approaching your position three miles out." The unspoken reality behind the order was obvious to everyone on the frequency. The ship couldn't afford to lose a fighter. A tanker, like the one I was now in, was more expendable. I had to ensure that priority and obey the command.

As Bob activated the transfer switch, all he and I could do was sit by in agonizing silence and watch our low-fuel light flash on at fourteen hundred pounds remaining, then drop to just below nine hundred pounds as the F-4 detached and headed for

Danang. With our fuel dangerously low, we had to descend and land immediately. There was no room for error. Jerking the jet down to approach altitude on instruments, I guided us into our final approach three miles behind the ship. In a driving rain, with horizontal visibility nil, the ship's controller began his rapid-fire instructions to get us on course and on glide path. Bob strained to see any sign of the ship while I locked on the instruments. All was not well. As we approached to inside a quarter mile, the LSO yelled, "Wave off, wave off! We can't see you."

I added full power and began a slight climb for safety. "Tighten your harness, Bob," I said. "We're out of here the moment the engine starts coughing." I knew that the only way we could survive ejection at sea was if plane guard helicopters or a destroyer found us, but only if they saw us eject, something I didn't care to think about.

While immediately commencing a left turn to make another attempt, I radioed the ship, "Three hundred fifty pounds, coming left." Extending downwind just briefly, I began a level turn at four hundred feet of altitude in the hopes that I could intercept a short glide slope for one last try. Rolling wings level, with the landing gear, flaps, and hook all set for landing, I decreased power slightly as the ship's controller called our distance. Inside a half mile, Bob caught a glimpse of the carrier's wake and then spotted the ship. Miraculously, it had steamed into a pocket of slightly clearer weather. With one quick adjustment on the throttles and the stick, I steered our gasping A-6 into the welcome grasp of the arresting wire on a thimble full of fuel.

Once clear of the landing area, I shut down the engines and tried to collect myself enough to climb out of the cockpit. Then, I walked off the flight deck with my visor still down and my knees shaking.

Fate hadn't been as kind to my colleagues during our tour in the Gulf of Tonkin. The commanding office of VA-93, one of two

A-7 light-attack jet squadrons in the airwing, had not returned from a multiple-plane day strike to Haiphong. An E-2B radar early-warning aircraft and its four crewmen had crashed into the sea during a night patrol. A ground-impact explosion had claimed the pilot of an F-8 Crusader during a supersonic photo-reconnaissance mission over Vinh. And an F-4J Phantom crew had been "bagged" by a surface-to-air missile near Nam Dinh.

Every casualty was a colleague, a roommate, or a dear friend. Ray Donnelly had been all of these to me. He had been flying a night strike in the "Hourglass" region north of Than Hoi on July 19 when a single-arms round penetrated the lower right-hand side of the plane's clear Plexiglas canopy and struck him in the neck. The force was so powerful, the bullet ripped through his ejection seat headrest and out the top of the canopy. Ray was courageous, respected, and dependable, and for the next few days his loss hovered over the squadron like a dark cloud. Placing his personal belongings in a gray metal box for shipment to his mother back home in Ohio had to be one of the most emotionally draining tasks any of us had ever faced.

Every few days, large canvas sacks were delivered during our at-sea replenishments from the various supply, ordnance, and fueling ships that came alongside the *Midway*. Among the small mountains of mail were envelopes addressed in familiar handwriting. Some were perfumed, and all demanded to be read. I could pull six g's with the best of my fellow pilots, but I could hardly pick up a letter opener and read the words of a wife who wanted me home. One line, repeated in almost every letter, kept me hoping: "Baby is growing. October 11 is our delivery date." I circled my calendar, unaware of the memory that date would hold.

Red-letter day

The war had begun to heat up. The U.S. State Department wanted to put increased pressure on the North Vietnamese peace talks, and the Air Force command center in Saigon had ordered our airwing to attack the Gia Lam railway complex just north of the Long Binh River in the center of Hanoi. Months of relentless, daily bombing runs against constant enemy fire raised our adrenaline to near-toxic levels. Too many missing flight crews had become permanent guests of the "Hanoi Hilton," and our squadron vowed that we were going to pay their North Vietnamese an unwelcome visit. This one would be for Ray Donnelly, Mike Bixel, and another dozen aviators in our airwing who would not return.

It would be remembered simply as the strike to Hanoi/Gia Lam. Our goal was to deposit seventy-five tons of bombs on a major North Vietnamese rail yard. Without electronic jamming support in the target area, our survival depended almost solely on our ability to evade enemy missiles and gunfire during our approach, attack, and egress. A low cloud cover had put a question mark on the mission. But the clouds parted, and we had a clear corridor all the way to Hanoi.

On the morning of our launch, sunlight sparkled off the opened canopies of the sleek, gray, swept-wing aircraft loaded with bombs, ammo cans, and missiles. Maintenance crews and plane captains, most of whom were barely beyond their teenage years and responsible for the readiness of multi-million-dollar aircraft, performed last-minute efforts to ensure the planes were ready. On this day their intensity seemed greater than ever. Red-shirted "ordies," who normally spent their final moments spray-painting endearing messages to Ho Chi Minh and his troops on the twenty-two olive green five-hundred-pound bombs, solemnly double-checked wing pylons and weapons fusing. Bob Ponton and I inspected the weathered skin of our

A-6 for any abnormalities or leaks, and then strapped into the side-by-side ejection seats.

During all of the preflight checks I could feel the sweat dripping off my forehead. The tension accelerated when my A-6 rocketed off the end of the flight deck at 165 knots, groped for altitude, then began its rock-steady climb. Minutes later, our strike group of twelve planes led by Commander Phil Gay, flying a VA-93 A-7 Corsair, rolled out on course, three miles high, toward the coastline of North Vietnam.

The usual headset chatter in my ears ceased. All radio communications had been silenced to delay enemy detection. Everything, from the formation to the flight profile, had been predetermined. The serenity in the cockpit and the modest radar static in our headsets belied the reality of the moment; we were fully armed and headed for trouble, and we all knew it. As experienced combatants, we were forced to summon every bit of ability, concentration, and courage to reach Hanoi, demolish the target, and return to the carrier with no losses.

It took less time to get to the coast-in-point than it does to write about it. Thirty miles offshore, as all twelve aircraft started a gradual descent toward twelve thousand feet, the enemy appeared right before our eyes and ears. The sharp rattlesnake sound in our headsets, and the flickering strobe lines on our radar detection scope, confirmed that our surprise mission was now over. The North Vietnamese were probing the skies for any inbound threat. And now they had sniffed us out.

We had never received a very warm reception from the gun and missile crews in Hai Doung. This day would not be any different. The North Vietnamese hadn't forgotten how to use their anti-aircraft artillery, as huge black and gray puffs of smoke laced the sky. Seconds later, the beet-red missile alert light began fluttering. The warning signal brayed like a French police car in hot pursuit, hammering my senses as we scanned the sky for the first missile threat.

"Switches break left! Break left!" The words screeched through my headset. One of the pilots had spotted the missiles. There they were, coming at us, on the left side of our strike group, two surface-to-air missiles, their long, white smoke trails marking a lethal trajectory toward the F-4 fighter/bombers. Within seconds another missile and smoke trail streaked by off to our right and exploded in the distance. No harm, no autopsy. Amazingly, the strike group held together. We were now minutes away from our target.

I could see the outskirts of Hanoi through the haze. Three minutes from roll-in, our A-6 section flight leader, XO Jack Presley, steered us slightly right to ensure we were offset at an appropriate distance north of the target for a left roll-in on the rail yard. I fine-tuned the bombsight illumination; I wanted to get the best possible view of the "pipper," the center point of the cross-hairs, that would signify the bomb-release point superimposed on the target at forty-five hundred feet. All this, while the sky around me darkened with enemy gunfire.

I looked down and saw the target. "I'm visual on the rail yard train repair building," I said to Bob. Twelve thousand feet below, I could see four North Vietnamese MiG-21 jets taxiing into take-off position on the adjacent airfield.

"Strike leader is in." As the command to attack shot through my headphones, Phil's A-7 pitched up slightly then snapped to the left and headed down. Seconds after three A-7s rolled in on the target, Presley followed suit. I counted "one thousand one, one thousand two," then jerked the A-6 into an identical trajectory, slightly offset to the right. As the nose approached forty-five degrees down, I rolled the wings upright.

The rail yard was in plain view. I could see the target appearing through the top of the bombsight, just a hair to the right. I streaked downward at seven hundred feet per second, as Bob called out our shrinking altitudes:

"Eight thousand. . . .

"Seven thousand. . . .

"Six thousand. . . .

"Five thousand. . . ."

At forty-five hundred feet, as the bombsight pipper tracked through the target, I depressed the red release button on the control stick. The aircraft shuddered as our twenty-two bombs rippled off the wing stations on their free fall to earth exactly as planned. We weren't done.

I snatched the stick to the right and began to pull out of the dive at five g's, the maximum amount of force the wings could bear at our speed. I didn't feel like flying through a fresh barrage of ground fire now blackening the sky all over Hanoi, so I banked sharply left and added full power. Yellow flashes and tracers streamed by on either side of the plane. Somehow, with enough jinking and twisting at five hundred knots, we made it.

With one final hard left turn, I looked back and saw the Gia Lam rail yard lost in a billow of thick, black smoke and three huge fires. The follow-on strike photography would report that fifteen major buildings were completely destroyed and that the railway trans-shipment facility, the hub that had been delivering an endless stream of weapons, equipment, and supplies to help feed North Vietnam's war machine, had been demolished.

While Gia Lam fell out of view, mayhem still reigned—not for moments but for minutes. Still in range of fire, we danced our planes through smoke, artillery bursts, and jet exhaust trails. None of us wanted to suffer the ultimate insult of being hit by enemy fire and ejecting over land.

The mission wasn't over until the flight commander said the magic words:

"Strike check." It was each pilot's cue to respond:

"Champs in trail."

"Raven's with three."

"Switchboxes up."

Everyone had made it! We had taken the heat of six missiles and what seemed like most of the North Vietnamese artillery arsenal. It was a red-letter day. That night on the flight deck during my night watch, the ship's chaplain handed me a slip of paper.

CONGRATULATIONS. YOUR WIFE HAD A HEALTHY BABY GIRL.
WEIGHT: 6 LBS. 1 OZ. SHANNON AND MOM DOING FINE.

On the piece of paper I wrote, "Shannon Leigh Horsley, October 10, 1972," and I put it in my stateroom safe with the few valuables I had onboard. I pictured the delivery room in Oak Harbor, Washington. I imagined a crying daughter and a tired, relieved mother, and I wondered when I would make it home.

Underneath my visor

As the war crept toward a slow, tiresome pullout of American forces, Vietnam attached itself to my memory bank:

• The night sky in Haiphong Harbor awash with green and white tracers aimed at the A-6 that Bob Ponton and I brought screaming in only two hundred feet over the water. Bob shrieks himself hoarse telling me to "Take it up! Take it up!" because without higher altitude, his radar won't find our target. Once I tell him to look outside, Bob pulls his head up from his navigator's screen, takes one look at the lethal green shower exploding directly out his window and then, in a moment of unscripted hilarity, betrays his navigator bias and yells, "Take it down! Take it down!"

• The sound of many twenty-one gun salutes provided during

our regular hangar deck memorial services for fellow aviators who hadn't returned.

• A drawer full of combat action awards that seemed meaningless in the context of the cost.

• A lifetime of midnight hamburgers and tasteless Kool-Aid.

• A photo of our squadron, including Mike Bixel, my roommate, whose aircraft's landing gear sheared off on a rainy nighttime landing, forcing him to eject as his burning jet slid down the flight deck, igniting an inferno. He, along with four others, died instantly. He was my roommate, my friend. Crew cut. Nice smile. Always steady, always there. Until that night.

There were two other pictures I took home from Vietnam. Two men who became more than roommates, more than friends. Mike McCormick and Arlo Clark. I had met both when I had joined VA-115 at Whidbey Island. Mike was a Notre Dame graduate with All-American good looks—dark curly hair, bubbly personality. The son of a Navy captain, he seemed to enjoy favored status and always seemed to be in the right place at the right time, doing everything the right way.

And then there was Arlo.

Irreverent. Always stirring the pot. Always with a suspect gleam in his eye. Not wild, but feisty. If you told him to do something, he'd look at you like you were crazy. As the most junior officer in the squadron, his "rookie initiation" assignment was to collect the ready room Teletype ticker tape that listed the steady stream of weather reports the ship received. While nobody ever intended to read it, it was Arlo's job to cut and paste this quarter-inch-wide paper trail into a logbook.

One night, a lull in the ready room was broken when Arlo walked in with a paper wad half the size of a basketball. "Who wants to look up the last four months of weather?" he beamed, as he bounced it off the floor.

Just like Mike Bixel and Ray Donnelly, Arlo was a bombardier/navigator. In January 1973, we could see the end coming in Vietnam. With only a few weeks left before our country ceased its military involvement in the war, Mike McCormick and Arlo Clark launched on a night strike against a heavily defended weapons facility northwest of Vinh.

They never came back.

Officially, they would be listed as "Missing In Action." When I heard the news, I insisted on flying the initial search-and-rescue flight. Just prior to dawn, two hours after they had failed to return from their ill-fated mission, I was airborne for their target area. I streaked deep into the thick cloud cover that obscured their intended flight route, oblivious to the threat of enemy weapons.

I picked up no radio signal from their emergency beacon or radios.

I found no trace of their aircraft.

For a moment in the cockpit, I was sitting again at Jackie Jensen's Restaurant in Oakland with Sonya, Arlo, and his wife, Tonya. We were smiling and laughing two days before heading into a war we barely understood.

Somewhere over North Vietnam, I stared straight ahead. Behind the dark helmet visor that shielded my face, I felt the tears pour down my cheeks. I couldn't stop them. For once, I didn't want to. I wept for Arlo and for Mike. I wept with bitterness over the death of two close friends and the senseless war I had somehow managed to survive.

How had I made it through?

The best I could come up with was that I had been, and still was, an ordinary individual who had been thrown into some extraordinary circumstances and that I had come out the other side feeling a sense of accomplishment—and sadness. I was now a more resilient, more self-determined man, not yet fully aware of what I had gained. And lost.

We returned to our home base at the Naval Air Station on Whidbey Island on a cold, gray afternoon, March 2, 1973, eleven months after leaving for Vietnam. Welcomed by the drums and bugles of a patriotic band and a bucket of champagne, I climbed out of my A-6 and renewed the reality of what things awaited—a wife who loved me, a daughter who captured my attention, and a son who grabbed me by the neck.

That afternoon, we commemorated our return and our losses by thundering over the base in a missing man formation. I returned from Vietnam as a proven warrior who had been successful beyond my wildest dreams. And I was still oblivious to how much higher I would climb, with my visor firmly in place.

4

"Up We Go!"

To those who have passed through and to those who shall follow,
the Blue Angels experience shall forever be a part of his or her life.
Certainly, it has been such with me.

—Roy "Butch" Voris
Captain, U.S. Navy (Ret.)
Founder, Blue Angels[1]

First came their flash. Then their thunder.

I could see their jet engine exhaust rippling the calm waters of Puget Sound a half mile offshore. Seconds later, the booming echo of a solo Blue Angel aircraft shook the ground around me. The sparkling blue A-4 Skyhawk screamed by at 450 knots, barely fifty feet overhead on its rifle-shot pass down the runway at the Whidbey Island Naval Air Station, before streaking toward the sky.

I stood on the seawall that cool afternoon in August 1975 and watched the Blue Angels perform a delicate aerial ballet of precision and speed. The "Blues," or Navy Flight Demonstration Squadron as they were officially known, comprised six of the finest pilots and over eighty of the best support personnel the Navy had to offer. I had seen them perform twice during my flight training days but with inexperienced eyes. Now, as a combat veteran and flight instructor with over three hundred carrier landings, I looked upward with added awe—and curiosity:

What would it take for me to fill a seat in one of those six jets?

Was I really good enough to match up with the ability and nerves required to fly an airshow of exacting maneuvers, wingtip to wingtip, at five hundred miles per hour? And could I repeat the feat for eighty different audiences a year?

Four years after admiring the world's most famous precision demonstration flight team in a new light on that sunlit afternoon on Whidbey Island, I continued to ask the question, "Could I? . . . Could I ever hack it as a Blue Angel?"

Since coming home from Vietnam in 1973, I had fattened my resumé. I had spent two years as an instructor pilot in A-6s and had started the A-6 medium attack warfare school, the A-6 equivalent of the Navy's "Top Gun" Fighter Weapons School.

After my tour with VA-128 ended, I had headed back to sea duty, this time as an admiral's aide on an aircraft carrier battle group staff. Sonya and I sold our home on Whidbey Island, packed up our belongings, two kids, and the dog, and relocated to Navy housing in Alameda, California. Most of the next two-year tour was spent at sea in support of a two-star admiral as I shifted from carrier to carrier in the western Pacific directing fleet and multi-national at-sea training exercises.

By December of 1978, I was back in Pensacola, where my naval aviation career began, instructing pilots in the TA-4J. This combat-capable, two-seat jet was truly a joy to fly. The downside was that my students included Kuwaiti Air Force pilots. Trying to demonstrate high-performance flight techniques to aviators who barely understood English, and who had very little background with technically complex aeronautical concepts, proved to be a steep challenge. Night formation flying took on a whole new dimension whenever a Kuwaiti pilot took his hands off the stick and screamed, "Allah will provide!"

It was no wonder that my attention soon turned to the sleek, blue and gold A-4 aircraft that shared maintenance space with our aging, oil-stained trainer jets. The contrast between the two squadrons couldn't have been more dramatic.

On one side of the hangar, my chief petty officer and I performed daily miracles trying to locate enough used equipment to keep most of our T-2s and TA-4s flying. The Blues, on the other hand, had a storeroom full of new equipment and extra supplies.

We could barely keep our planes flyable let alone keep them clean. The Blues' aircraft were all hand waxed.

Our maintenance people were mostly new recruits and inexperienced sailors. The Blues' enlisted crews were all handpicked, seasoned veterans.

Our flight attire consisted of baggy olive-green jumpsuits and cumbersome, scuffed boots. The Blues wore tight-fitting tailored blue and gold flight suits and spit-shined, lightweight half boots. It didn't take much for me to know which squadron the Navy valued more. The opportunity was obvious. I had a choice to make: Which career move would allow me to get to the top?

Money-wise, it was a no-brainer. As an admiral's aide, I had made new friends in the San Francisco business community. With these contacts, the doors to a real estate or business career seemed wide open. I could enjoy more income, less danger, and more time at home with Sonya, Jeff, and Shannon, who had become accustomed to celebrating birthdays, anniversaries, and holidays alone. Logically, financially, and realistically, I had every reason to leave the Navy, except one, and that was the memory of a blue and gold jet streaking across the sky on a sunlit afternoon. Every time I was in the hangar, I gazed past our squadron aircraft to the A-4s assigned to the Blue Angels. I looked at the hand-scripted names of each pilot painted on their respective planes:

Commander Bill "Boss" Newman
Lieutenant Commander Mike Nord
Lieutenant Commander Bruce Davey
Lieutenant Commander Jerry Tucker

I stared at the names and I wondered. . . . In nine years of Navy aviation I had become a highly decorated combat veteran. I had received a raft of excellent performance evaluations. And I had developed an impressive network of Navy captains and admiral flag officer sponsors willing to endorse my future.

I knew Sonya was reveling in the daily luxury of welcoming me home at regular hours. After eight homes in nine years, she liked the thought of a familiar zip code and a semi-normal home life. For her the future held the hope of satisfying friendships and a stable family. I had other things on my mind. Standing inside the hangar in Pensacola, surrounded by a sea of spare parts and a handful of jets I could fly only so fast and so far, I made a major flight correction.

I decided to apply to become a Blue Angel.

I knew I couldn't do it on my own. The Navy had to officially sanction my availability to apply for the team, and applicants were not in short supply. I would be competing against some sixty other highly qualified naval aviators for the two flight positions and one narrator job. The Navy okayed my application, and by the end of that summer I wound up on a short list of finalists still being considered for the three coveted open slots.

The selection would be made on attributes related to combat and general aviation reputation, carrier landing performance, leadership ability, personality, image, public relations, and commitment to teamwork. In reality, the final criterion was how well the applicant could relate personally to the other Blue Angel team members during a grueling, relentless air show schedule and how well he could handle the stress that comes from always being "on stage" in a very high-performance environment.

Over the next few weeks, I developed a deep appreciation for the Blues, particularly how they were founded. In 1946, Roy "Butch" Voris, a twenty-five-year U.S. Navy lieutenant commander had been selected to put together a flight exhibition team. His only directive was that the team's purpose was to perform at air shows and other public events. From the first demonstrations that lasted seventeen minutes in four Hellcats, the Blue Angels had built an unrivaled reputation for precision and close-formation flying throughout North America.

The application process had gone on for nearly three months. It was now late September, notification week for those who would be selected to join the Blues for the coming 1980 season. I had to get away from the constant questioning of friends at the squadron. So, after lunch I went home to do a few projects. That afternoon, the phone rang.

Before lifting the receiver, I had a good idea who it was.

"Hello, Jim Horsley speaking."

"Jim this is Nordo." Mike Nord was the current left wingman. "Jim, this is not a call I want to make. . . . " One by one, the current Blue Angel team members came on the line to offer me their condolences for my having come so close, yet not making the cut. Disappointment welled up in my throat. As I began to stammer for a response, the flight leader, Commander Bill Newman, interrupted.

"Congratulations, Jim. Welcome aboard! You are the new left wingman, number three, for the 1980 team!" The "Boss" then ticked off the rest of my new team members and their respective positions. I don't think I heard him say one name. I was too elated, too astounded.

Jim Horsley:

> Flailing childhood swimmer.
> Five-foot eight-inch junior high power forward.
> Former pyromaniac.
> Wide-eyed A-5 admirer.
> Blue Angel.

When I hung up the phone, the sobering responsibility of my new role hit home. Throughout the selection process I had projected a sense of confidence. All my talk was now wasted air. My performance, as a Blue Angel, would be all that mattered. I merely had to prove that I could become an integral part of the best precision flight demonstration team in the world.

So close, so fast

Within a month, I turned over my VT-4 responsibilities, walked across the hangar, and reported for duty with the Blue Angels. Early the next week, neatly attired in a spare blue flight suit, I experienced my first flight with the Blues.

It was mid-week in Pensacola, and that meant yet another practice routine for the Blues. Only this time would be different. I would be in the back seat of the Blues' two-seat TA-4J for an orientation flight. Bruce Davey would give me a bird's-eye view of a typical air show while flying in the slot position directly behind the flight leader. Bruce, or "Squire," as he was known by his teammates, was in his third year with the Blue Angels. He had served as the narrator in his first year, flew left wing the second, and now was flying as number four. A polished aviator, outspoken in his pursuit for perfection for the Blues, Squire had a penchant for practical jokes and commanded extraordinary respect from the rest of the team.

Each of us had been tagged with a unique call sign, and it didn't take long for the team to start calling me "Nag," a rather unflattering takeoff on "Horsley," which, obviously, was harder to say quickly on the radio. "Nag" or not, I was about to get a first-class demo.

My carefully measured, subdued comments while manning up the aircraft were in sharp contrast to my pounding heart and sweaty palms. The takeoff checklist rolled by:

> "Smoke pressure on. . . .
> "Altimeter 29.97. . . .
> "Check trim at one degree nose up/roll in the feel. . . .
> "Head knockers up. . . .
> "Spoilers de-armed. . . ."

We taxied toward the runway in section, two planes side-by-side. My first impression wasn't that I was now a Blue Angel, or that I was sitting in the rear cockpit with a veteran pilot in front of me. My only thought was that our plane's wingtip was just about touching Nordo's number three jet leading our section!

"There's no way you can taxi this close to a guy without hitting him," I said to myself.

At the hold short end of the runway, we closed up with the "Boss" and Fred "Stank" Stankovich, in Blue Angel jets one and two. Bruce turned the airplane until we were almost perpendicular with the runway. With the engines whining, and the four planes creeping to a stop, the nose of our airplane nudged into the horizontal stabilizer of Nordo's plane.

Without missing a beat, Squire called out on the radio, "Oops, got you first." I was astonished. Apparently this wasn't unusual.

In eleven years of flying, I had yet to put a scratch on an airplane, much less hit one.

We boomed down the runway and took off into a Diamond formation high-performance climb that culminated with a wingover, then descended back down to one thousand feet for our transit to the outlying practice field thirty miles to the east. Bruce effortlessly put the plane through its paces, and with each turn or bank the aircraft stayed locked in position behind the flight leader.

Slipping to the outside of the formation, and thirty feet down the left wing line of Mike Nord in number three, Squire keyed the intercom and said, "Nag, you've got the stick. Take it in to whatever distance you like."

This was my chance to show him what I could do. The air speed indicator read 350 knots. I turned my focus to Nord's left wing, then gently adjusted the controls. Our plane crept closer to the neighboring A-4 until I felt I was stabilized at the correct distance. We were six feet from the other plane. "Why quit now?" I thought. I could do better.

I gently moved the stick, and our plane crept a few more inches closer. I congratulated myself. Five feet. That should do it.

"You think that's about it?" Squire asked.

"I'll move it in another foot," I said, without even a whisper of bravado in my voice.

"I've got it," he said. And then, while maintaining our speed, Bruce deftly drove our airplane to within three feet of the other plane's wingtip. I didn't have words to describe the scenery, because I couldn't catch my breath. Sitting in the backseat, I was mesmerized by Nordo's right wingtip dancing a scant thirty-six inches from Bruce's helmet. I was close enough to count the rivets on the skin of the airplane. Then it began to dawn on me that this is where I'm going to be flying the coming year during eighty air shows—on the left wing, three feet from the flight leader's left wingtip, at speeds from 120 to 480 knots, supposedly locked into this position.

As I was trying to comprehend this reality, Bruce said, "Remember this picture, because it's where you're going to be living for the next year." I honestly didn't know how I would ever fly so close, and so fast. However, for the next couple of months of training, I came to realize that Bruce wasn't lying.

Rare Diamond

Two flights a day, seven days a week, for six weeks. From early January to mid-March, the Blue Angels' winter training consumed nearly every waking moment. The site was the Naval Air Facility at El Centro, California, in the Imperial Valley, about one hundred miles east of San Diego. Our entire team, including the eighty-man crew of hand-selected maintenance, administrative, and support personnel arrived in "Fat Albert," a C-130 transport that also carried miscellaneous spare equipment and supplies. Our agenda was simple: learn, practice, and perfect a forty-minute air show that, according to our press releases, "would demonstrate precision naval aviation techniques for the American public."

We had forty-two days to make it happen before our initial air show at the Marine Corps Air Station in Yuma, Arizona, on March 15. Every hour of every day was designed to prepare us mentally and physically. The centerpiece of our daily regimen was two eighty-minute training flights. Each time up, what made it fun was the jet that carried us.

The single-seat, single-engine A-4F Skyhawk, affectionately nicknamed "Scooter" by those who flew it, was the sports car of military jet aircraft. Designed by Ed Heineman of the Douglas Aircraft Company and first flown in 1954, "Heineman's Hotrod" was forty-two feet long and could fly at speeds of 550 knots. It had been designed as a safe, low-cost carrier-based Navy light attack aircraft that would provide great maneuverability, reliability, and weapons flexibility in a target area. Carrying a mix of five-hundred- to one-thousand-pound bombs, rockets, and cannons, the "Scooter" packed a punch. Outside of combat, the A-4's maneuverability was exceptional. Its roll rate was dizzying. Deflecting the stick fully to the left or right caused the airplane to roll two revolutions in one second.

The A-4's cockpit was snug for my nearly six-foot frame but nearly claustrophobic for anyone over six feet tall. Bob Stephens, who joined the Blues in my second year, and who stood six feet five inches, probably concluded that the plane's designer had dwarfs on his mind when he tried to squeeze into the modest cockpit.

The A-4's diminutive size belied its in-flight capabilities. It could carry enough fuel for two hours of normal operation. In order to ensure maximum performance for our air shows, we minimized the plane's weight and only loaded it with enough fuel to take us through the air show, plus a ten-minute reserve.

Most impressive, though, was the A-4's power plant. The Pratt and Whitney P-408 engine provided exceptional acceleration. At low fuel loads, the Skyhawk had nearly a one-to-one thrust-to-weight ratio, which meant that at low altitudes, the plane could sustain vertical nose-up flight without losing any airspeed, an exceptional feat for a subsonic aircraft.

Unique modifications to the aircraft enabled the Blues to pull off our demanding maneuvers. The leading edge slats, for instance, which would normally extend by gravity at reduced airspeeds during takeoffs and landings, were bolted closed and dipped in chrome to reduce drag and improve their appearance. The oil pump was specially designed to operate during sustained inverted flight. And the wing pylons, designed to carry weapons or extra fuel tanks, were removed to streamline the wings.

When it came to sheer aerial showmanship, one tiny refinement was the plane's coup de grace. Designers installed an additional oil tank near the plane's tail that connected to a quarter-inch-diameter vent tube. At the appropriate moment in each maneuver, the flight leader would call, "Smoke on." At the *n* of *on*, each pilot would flip a switch on the left side of the throttle, sending oil into the jet engine exhaust. A thick stream of white smoke would then pour out the back of each plane. This bit of flare underlined the showmanship that crowds everywhere came to expect from the Blues.

The A-4's most impressive refinement, however, was tucked out of view. Because we flew in such tight formation, the slightest stick movements had to produce a corresponding change in pitch or roll. Unlike a steering wheel on a car, which even at seventy miles per hour can be moved slightly without affecting the direction, the Blue Angels needed precise responsiveness. Navy technical representatives from McDonnell-Douglas came up with the solution when they attached an artificial-feel spring bungee to the control linkage. This eliminated any "play" in the stick, so that even the slightest movement of the stick made the plane respond immediately. When activated by a switch on the stick grip, the spring pulled the stick forward, almost to the instrument panel.

Prior to takeoff, I would "roll in the feel," then pull the stick backward into the neutral position with my right arm—and hold it there for the entire flight. After maintaining twenty pounds of pull for forty-five minutes, my right forearm felt like a rock. It was a small price to pay for the challenge and thrill that awaited me in the air.

The daily training regimen began at five o'clock each morning. After a breakfast of microwaved oatmeal, granola bars, and coffee, our team of six gathered at a cold government-issue gray table in the quiet confines of the squadron briefing room. There, we covered every aspect of the pending flight. Nothing escaped our attention: weather and wind conditions, specific sequence procedures, maneuver refinement techniques, safety reminders, and voice calls.

The forty-minute air show sequence consisted of a combination of twelve Diamond (four-plane) formation maneuvers alternating with twelve Solo opposing/head-on passes. The air show culminated with six Delta (six-plane) formation rolling/looping maneuvers. Every turn, every bank, every straight pass was analyzed on the ground by a dozen pair of eyeballs, and a video camera that never blinked. Following each flight, we spent an hour scrutinizing every aspect of the video and personal observations of the just-completed practice routine.

Commander Denny Wisely, who had replaced Commander Newman as the "Boss," would lead off the general comments for the debrief.

"Felt a little rough from my cockpit. . . .

"Late up on the Diamond roll. . . .

"Good adjustments behind the flight line for the Diamond loop. . . ."

The rest of us would then chip in with our observations and comments in sequence. In these meetings, pride took a backseat to constructive critique. Anyone who thought, "If that's what I did, that's what I intended to do," didn't gain much sympathy or agreement.

With our minds fully awake and dawn beginning to break in the eastern sky, we pushed our chairs back from the table and headed to the hangar to sign the aircraft maintenance logbooks. Then at sunup, with every salute, step, and sequence slaved to precision, our blue A-4s would thunder off the runway for another practice.

Though the individual maneuvers changed each day during winter training, our approach did not.

Observe. Study. Adjust.

Focus. Execute. Repeat.

Commit it all to memory, then commit yourself to making it perfect in the air.

Throughout the six weeks at El Centro, we took only one day off every two weeks. The remaining hours were filled with twice-a-day briefings, flights, debriefs, studying, exercising, early dinners—and amazement.

I thought back to my demonstration ride the first time I saw Nordo's left wing just thirty-six inches from my helmet. After the first week of training, what I once thought impossible seemed within arm's reach, literally! Though we didn't start our training with a wingtip-to-canopy separation of thirty-six inches, we made it our goal. It wasn't easy. Positioning six Navy jets in the same airspace that close together and still safely roll, shift forma-tions, and cross paths did not happen in one flight, one week, or one month.

The balanced Diamond formations, Left and Right Echelon formations, line abreast loops, "dirty rolls" with the landing gear and arresting hooks down, fan break, and tuck-under break maneuvers all demanded unique position adjustments and for-mation changes. With no time to either congratulate or doubt ourselves, we practiced each maneuver, fighting turbulence and sun glare, determined to keep the airplanes absolutely riveted in position.

Everyone in the Diamond formation had unique responsibili-ties, with the Boss's probably the most difficult. He needed to place each formation maneuver at the exact airspeed, altitude, and angle in relation to our flight line center point located fifteen hundred feet in front of, and parallel to, the crowd. (This point was usually a fire truck centered on the outboard edge of the runway, or a point marked by anchored boats in over-water shows.) Each of the maneuvers needed to be at the correct timing interval following the prior maneuver so that our "flow" was consistent during the air show. Voice calls, smooth stick and throttle adjustments, and cloud avoidance were equally important, and it would take a new "Boss" months to assimilate all of it into a fluid performance.

In the Diamond Roll, when the lead Solo called, "Solo's clear" on his Knife Edge opposing pass at four hundred knots and one hundred feet down the flight line, the Boss needed to have the Diamond formation in a descending left-hand turn about two miles from center point to the crowd's right. The hardest work actually took place behind the crowd, as we "eased" the set, or distance, between aircraft to about five feet following each maneuver while the Boss would aggressively guide the formation in the necessary high-g climbs, descents, and turns to get set up for the next maneuver in the air show sequence. Each movement of his aircraft was predicated by a voice call to ensure we knew exactly what he was about to do with his stick or power.

The Diamond Roll exemplified the need for exact precision. From the crowd's perspective, the maneuver moved from right to left. The four-plane formation would begin to climb and, on signal from the Boss, roll 360 degrees until leveling off at the same original altitude. Done correctly, the crowd would see four planes that appeared welded together. Achieving this goal was easier said than done.

As the Boss called, "Go Diamond," we would smoothly shift back into tight formation from our "eased out" formation behind the crowd. Nordo, flying directly below and behind the Boss's tailpipe in number four, would call, "You've got four, Boss." This indicated our four jets were now in the correct Diamond position. Stank, on the right wing in number two, would establish his "set" at the proper bearing and thirty-six inches from the Boss's right wingtip. My job in number three was to ensure that my position on the Boss's left wing matched Stank's. I would use peripheral vision to verify, but at no time could I afford to move my focus away from the Boss's plane. As the Boss called, "We're in a descending turn for the Diamond Roll," each of us, in staccato fashion, would acknowledge with our call sign: "Stank." "Nag." "Nordo." This indicated to the Boss that we were in position, that radios were working, and that we each were anticipating the correct maneuver.

The formation was now descending and accelerating to a pull-up altitude of two hundred feet at 350 knots, with an inboard-to-outboard "cut" on the flight line of about thirty degrees.

"Rolling out the Diamond Roll" indicated that we were approaching our pull-up heading. Then came the commands:

> "Wings level."
> "Smoke on."
> "Up we go."

At the *w* of *we*, all four pilots in the Diamond would, in unison, apply smooth back-stick pressure such that the formation stayed locked in position as we began our upward climb. As we approached thirty-five degrees nose up, the Boss would call, "O . . . kay," and at the *k* the formation would commence a left roll, each pilot maintaining the exact relative position on the Boss's jet.

At that point, Nordo, in the slot, needed to "cheat" slightly to the right to ensure that the crowd's perspective still showed a symmetrical Diamond. At the same time, he would check our altitude and air speed as a backup to the Boss to ensure we were rolling fast enough with enough altitude to safely complete the roll. The Boss would continue the roll to achieve inverted flight as our noses passed through the horizon before completing the roll and leveling off at the same altitude and air speed at which we started.

"Smoke off."

"Easing the pull."

"Adding Power. . . . Adding more power."

"Coming left for the Diamond Loop."

"Stank." "Nag." "Nordo."

And for the next fifteen maneuvers, we repeated the cycle.

Each maneuver was scrutinized. During our debrief, the squadron maintenance officer, Ben Woods, and flight surgeon, "Doc" Charlie Thomason, offered maneuver-by-maneuver critique. On a Diamond Roll, one of them might say, "Rough wings on the 'up.' Apex of the roll too far left. High finish." We would grump about their lack of visual acuity, then watch the video and know they were absolutely right.

From the ground, our formations appeared smooth and flawless. The view from inside the cockpit, however, was anything but tranquil. As the left wingman, the Boss's wingtip wiggled in front of my face, and it took an extra measure of determination and focus not to flinch while working to stay in position. Turbulence could shake the plane like a tambourine, and occasionally our planes swapped paint.

During every training flight we sought perfection. Yet, every maneuver, every climb carried the possibility of a catastrophe. We did everything we could to assuage the risk. But the stark reality was always there. Besides, we all knew the stories. In early 1973, when the Blues were still flying F-4J Phantoms, three of the four aircraft in formation collided in a trail loop during winter training. The desert floor outside of El Centro, the same proving ground for our team of six, became littered with the jets' twisted remains. Fortunately, all three pilots ejected to safety.

Later that same year, Blue Angel pilot Skip Umstead was leading a four-plane Diamond Roll during arrival maneuvers at Lakehurst, New Jersey, when, at the bottom of the maneuver, his F-4 slammed into trees. Skip, a crew chief in the rear seat, and wingman Mike Murphy were killed. The remainder of that season's air show schedule was cancelled.

The mental readiness required to fly with the Blues was not that different from how I approached air strikes or carrier landings. Other than an occasional gulp after a near miss, I didn't allow myself to dwell on the downside.

In my mind, it all came down to self-determination. Absolute concentration was mandatory. Tolerance for distractions—a stray thought, a twitching nose hair, a sneeze—was non-existent. My thinking had to be totally trained to anticipate the next voice call, stick movement, and formation maneuver. The cost of not doing so was painfully unacceptable.

I didn't feel courageous or heroic. I simply accepted the risk of flying close to the flame. The possibility of danger didn't threaten me; rather it warmed me to the task. And still, I pushed myself to fly along that fine line that represented the difference between maximum performance and disaster.

After Vietnam, I knew I wasn't invincible. Yet, while I was aware of my own mortality, my safety depended upon my ability. All six pilots took the same attitude. The only way we could survive our high-wire aerial act was to have exceptional confidence in ourselves and in each other. I had to depend on the fact that each of the other pilots knew exactly what he needed to do and that he could be relied on to make every turn, every climb, consistently without error. We had unwavering trust in each other despite knowing that any one of us was capable of making a fatal mistake. As a result, we became relentless in our demands of one another. Tension, exhaustion, and unrealistic expectations of each others' performance could chafe at large egos and ignite tempers.

It usually showed up in our debriefs. Nordo, as safety observer in the formation, would say, "Boss, we can't hang on with your erratic wing movements rolling out the loop."

"Then adjust the set," fired back Commander Wisely, who was dealing with his own frustration in trying to fly the proper profiles and didn't have the formation perspective that Nordo did in the slot.

Disagreements were ironed out, and grudges were never allowed beyond closed doors. Our very survival in mid-air required total trust, and that meant individual tempers took a backseat to renewed cooperation and teamwork. To help ensure our physical and mental health, "Doc" Thomason also served as mediator, treating injurious comments and massaging bruised egos back into shape.

By the end of February, we were counting the hours until our opening air show in Yuma. Not only did we have to perfect our "high" show for clear-sky days, but we also put together a routine that allowed us to fly a "low" show when cloud layers precluded us from doing looping maneuvers. We could fly a "flat" show that enabled us to perform with cloud cover as low as one thousand feet. Each format demanded total, instant recall of all eighteen formation maneuvers.

Gradually, with the Diamond formation and solos working on separate routines, maneuvers, and sequences, we began to achieve air show quality in our practice performances. We narrowed our wingtip-to-canopy separation distance in the Diamond formation from four to three feet. Our bottom altitudes, ideally two hundred feet, were consistent at three hundred and improving. Our final task was to integrate the Diamond and solos into our six-plane, forty-minute routine, including five "Delta" maneuvers that culminated in a high-speed flat pass and a six-plane formation landing. This we accomplished in the last ten days. Our "final exam" was a practice show over the base at El Centro for a number of the local residents who had treated us like family for the previous two months. Though not perfect, it was consistent and safe, and it looked and felt like an air show.

By Thursday, March 13, we were tanned, trained, and ready to be turned loose to show our stuff. On a gusty, warm afternoon we said good-bye to El Centro and pointed our jets east for the short seventy-mile transit to Yuma, where we boomed down toward the city bloated with "snowbirds." Our six polished A-4s descended to three hundred feet in Delta formation. Our flight leader in Blue Angel one, Denny Wisely, having earned his title of "Boss," called, "Wings level, a little drive. . . . Smoke on." My left pinky flipped the switch at the same instant as my five fellow pilots, and six trails of white smoke poured from the tails of six streaking jets now flying as one.

Smoke and thunder

The air station in Yuma, as in all of the seventy-nine other cities that would host the Blue Angels that year, became a perpetual roar at the next day's air show. Military jets, stunt aerobatics teams, wing-walkers, ultra-lights, helicopters, and restored military fighters bombarded the crowd with engines screaming at full power. The crowd spread out like a small temporary city filled with T-shirt vendors, souvenir booths, and always, the portable chemical toilets.

The free-form proceedings changed when the six of us, dressed in sharply creased blue flight suits, snapped to attention on the flight line. After gathering at the narrator's stand, we conducted our "walk down" to the jets. With our pre-flight briefing behind us, we steeled ourselves for the business at hand.

Casual chatter gave way to private thoughts. This prelude to takeoff, stepping in formation toward the planes was the only time I ever felt nervous. Occasionally, there would be some last-minute distraction from the FAA. With a simple "Let's go" from the Boss, we assembled in formation near Blue Angel number one. An expectant hush settled and then the narrator shattered the quiet with, "Good afternoon Ladies and Gentlemen. Since 1946 the Navy Flight Demonstration Squadron has. . . ."

We stepped out in unison, side by side, and marched toward the jets, precisely aligned wingtip to wingtip facing the crowd. As we approached the nose of our respective planes we peeled off, then circled around and behind the aircraft to the stainless steel ladder leading up to the cockpit. Every movement was timed to coincide with the narrator's description. As I started up the ladder, then swung my right leg over the canopy rail, the narrator said, "Flying Blue Angel number four, from Billings, Montana, Lieutenant Commander Jim Horsley."

I settled into the ejection seat. Within seconds, I pulled off my uniform hat and ascot and neatly stowed them in a pouch on the left side of the cockpit. My crew chief, Keith Hulbert, had already scrambled up the ladder behind me. As soon as I slipped the seat harness over both shoulders, he handed me the form-fitted yellow-gold flight helmet. It slid comfortably into place like an old shoe. Then I quickly slid the gold-plated visor down across my face and adjusted the attached microphone so that it just touched my upper lip. I was ready for engine start.

I took one last glance at the crowd. I savored the moment, as each person strained for a better look at what would come next. In the faces of many of the men I could see a little boy secretly aspiring to do what I was doing. I smiled, not out of superiority, but because I knew the speed and power of the pending performance would leave most of them speechless.

Once each pilot was nestled inside, the countdown began. A pitched-whine of Blue Angel number one's engine pierced the air. Then number two. Then number three. On cue from my crew chief, I positioned the necessary switches to start my engine and turn the electrical power on.

The flight leader initiated radio check-in on a discreet frequency. "Boss is up."

The calls rippled back.

"Stank."

"Nag."

"Nordo."

"Jungle."

"Elk."

The next call crackled in my headset. "Smoke on." Simultaneously, all six of us flipped on the smoke switch, then switched it off at "Smoke off." On the Boss's next command of "Canopies . . . closed" we pulled our canopies down with our left hands and prepared to taxi.

We rolled out in two-plane sections, first the Boss, and Stank in Blue Angel number two. I added power as they moved past my nose, then I taxied out behind them thirty feet in trail as Nordo slid in tightly on my right wing.

The Solos rolled out thirty feet behind us as we allowed our speed to increase toward the end of the takeoff runway. The collective thunder and intimate proximity of the six airplanes impressed the crowd to no end.

We adjusted positions as we taxied onto the runway and stopped. "Diamond Takeoff High-Performance Climb, right turn out," called the Boss.

For two months we had listened to his voice. We had grown to anticipate it, to respond to it, and to trust it.

"Run 'em up," the Boss called. Simultaneously, with each of us applying leg-shaking brake pressure with each foot on top of the rudder pedals, we all quickly advanced the throttles to stabilize the straining engines at 80 percent power. Checking engine instruments and flight controls for free movement, we each signaled a thumbs-up to the Boss.

"Off brakes . . . now!" At the *n* of *now*, each pilot released his brakes.

Exactly one second later we added additional power to match the Boss's engine and raced down the runway.

Seconds later we were airborne.

With our landing gear retracted, the Boss called, "Up we go!" And with that, he rotated up into an ever-increasing vertical climb.

Smoke and thunder followed.

Jim Ross, the lead solo pilot, was now into his "dirty roll." And then Jack Ekl and his Half-Cuban Eight/High-Speed Pass, ripping down the flight line past the crowd at five hundred miles per hour.

The air show was on. We were on our way, soaring to perfection.

Unless the unthinkable happened.

5

The Perfect Air Show

A hush, then a sigh, as the violence cried,
in the roar and the whine of the planes.
And the people who gasped as the thunder had
passed now watch as the sound slowly wanes.

If asked they'd reply with a gleam in their eye
that they came to watch rhythm and grace.
That the beauty of flight is important to see
and "Oh, what I'd give for your place."

But in truth what they want is death closely lit,
though clothed in respectable dress,
And if darkness then swallows the lamplighters'
flame the pleasure is greater not less.

So bring on the men and their flying machines,
let caution be left to the lame.
But remember the crowd doesn't care if you burn
so fly not too close to the flame.

—BRUCE DAVEY
LIEUTENANT COMMANDER, U.S. NAVY[1]

On good days, the air show became a graceful ballet. Sometimes in bad weather, it felt like we were wearing Norwegian clogs. Yet, we always kept dancing. For thirty-two consecutive weekends, from March to November, for forty minutes at a time, and

81

to the fascination and delight of sun-baked audiences, our aerial demonstration team of six played with fire. I never allowed myself to think about touching the flame. At least not during my first year.

Best seat in the house

The air show ritual always began with a precision-like rush and six claps of blue thunder. Before people could tilt their binoculars skyward, we were already setting up for the Head-On. All six planes swung wide until we were perpendicular to the flight line. Then, seemingly from nowhere, we flew directly toward the sea of spectators. The two Solos on the outposts of our six-plane Delta formation broke off. Our remaining foursome roared over the ear drums and sun visors at one thousand feet below.

But the Solos weren't done. Back they came, this time from opposite directions, screaming toward the flight line—and at each other. Racing at a Blue Angel pedestrian speed of 350 knots, and at one hundred feet off the ground in full view of the crowd, the two planes passed in front of the crowd seemingly nose-to-nose. In their millisecond meeting, only ten feet separated the two planes.

We were just warming up.

Moments later, the four-plane Diamond twisted right for spacing, then reversed hard left for the Diamond 360. This sweeping eighty-degree left bank, circular, right-to-left pass one hundred feet above the runway gave the crowd a slow-speed, close-up view of the four jets locked together.

From there, we clicked off the maneuvers:

The Knife Edge two-plane Solo pass, a move that looks like it was inspired by a mid-air collision.

The four-plane Diamond Loop that produced a four-g force for each pilot as he rounded the bottom side of the loop.

The Left Echelon Roll, a four-plane, corkscrew-like move the books say cannot be done, unless you performed it daily.

At twenty- to twenty-five-second intervals, the display of speed, noise, and tight formations bombarded the crowd. For them, the air show was sheer amazement. For me, it was a pulsing adrenaline gland.

In my first year, as the left wingman, I concentrated entirely on staying locked in the correct position for each maneuver. Each formation, each roll, each caress of the stick that nudged my plane within inches of a neighboring jet, demanded total focus. In that first year, what mattered most was how well I maintained position. Fred Stankovich, the right wingman, established the "set," and I matched him. I kept my head down and my eyes wide open. It was all I could do to simply stay with the team. If I flew a consistent, stable formation during the air show, I felt I had done my job.

All of that changed during my second year on the team.

In the natural progression of positions, I became the slot pilot. Nestled behind and below the flight leader's tail pipe, I had the best seat in the house for the air show. In a way, I felt like a season-ticket holder whose seats had been upgraded. In my first year as left wingman on the backside of a loop, I had become used to looking at rivets on the underside of the leading edge slat of the Boss's plane next to me. In my second year, the view out my canopy widened dramatically. As we would complete the bottom of a 360-degree loop at four hundred knots, I looked peripherally through the formation and saw the ground, the crowd line, and the entire expanse of the air show.

Such panoramic views were secondary to a new, more demanding role. As the slot pilot, I became responsible for the positioning and safety of all four planes in the Blues' Diamond formation. I let the flight leader know how the formation was hanging together, then radioed any necessary adjustments.

All it took was a single phrase. "Move the set up a scosh, Wiz."

"Roger that," said new Marine Corps right wingman, Tim Dineen, and it was done. Within seconds, new left wingman, Bob Stephens, matched the distance to ensure aerial symmetry. In turbulence, when the airplanes bounced like ducks in a shooting gallery, I calmly said, "Ease the set, Wiz. Let's not bang any wing tips."

Anticipate, assess, act. It was the only way we could maintain the thin cushion of air between the airplanes that represented the difference between maximum performance and disaster.

In my second year, I flew with a new perspective. Instead of seeing six individual airplanes, instead of thinking mostly about my own performance, I looked at the Blue Angels as one, unified team. It was no longer a matter of "me," but "we." Throughout that second season, I kept asking myself, "Are we maintaining the Blue Angel tradition? Are we performing at the ultimate level for ourselves and the crowd?"

Two things drove my desire. Most importantly, I wanted to ensure the team's complete safety. And yet I wanted something more. I wanted to perform flawlessly. I wanted this group of Blue Angels, I wanted our team, to fly the perfect air show. To a man, all six of us believed it was possible. It meant each pilot executing all eighteen maneuvers and the thousands of stick and throttle movements precisely the way we had been trained. To me, it was just a matter of time.

Finally, on one particular Saturday afternoon, I felt perfection within our grasp.

Graduation day

In the category of "Audience You Would Most Like to Impress," the only nominee was Annapolis, Maryland. Normally, this quiet little city would not qualify as an air show site for the Blue Angels, except that it just happens to be the home of the United States Naval Academy. On graduation day, May 25, we were the featured performers. If ever there was a time to shine before the Navy's top brass and future officers, this was it.

At 2:45 that afternoon, I marveled at the view enshrouding my canopy. In a gentle, arcing turn for the Head-On, six jets sparkled in the sunlight on our descent to two hundred feet. With vapor slipping off the wings, we were virtually welded as one:

Commander Denny Wisely, United States Navy, Commanding Officer/Flight Leader, plane number one.

Major Tim Dineen, United States Marine Corps, Right Wing, plane number two.

Lieutenant Commander Bob Stephens, United States Navy, Left Wing, plane number three.

Along with the solo pilots—Lieutenant Commanders Jack Ekl and Stu Powrie—the six of us represented a combined total of nineteen thousand flight hours, including twenty-two hundred carrier landings. But perhaps more significantly, we had trained and flown together for nearly two hundred days, refining and perfecting our air show. I knew what each man had sacrificed in terms of marriage, family, and frayed nerve endings to fly with the Blues. I knew that each hated mediocrity and hungered for excellence. And I felt privileged to count myself in their company.

The air show at Annapolis began flawlessly. Each fly-by, each setup, each turn, flowed together in a sweet, natural rhythm. Thirty minutes into the show, everything was falling into place. Even the Double Farvel, in which the flight leader and I flew upside down sandwiched between the two wingmen three feet to either side, in a level pass at three hundred feet, was impeccable. After getting the toughest diamond maneuvers behind us, the air show felt seamless.

Only ten minutes more remained. Four more maneuvers and

we were home. This was the perfect air show all of us knew we could do. Following our six-plane Delta formation roll, we completed a nose-high reversal turn and rolled back out on the flight line headed into the "Fleur De Lis," a modified looping maneuver in which the formation separated on the up, and then came back together on the backside.

Following the Boss's command, "Up we go," the formation began a two-g climb toward vertical. Thirty degrees nose up. The Boss called, "Ready break . . . ready roll," and all six jets pulled away from each other slightly then broke into dramatic 360-degree rolls. The Solos completed their rolls and thundered on past the crowd in level flight while the four diamond jets continued our climb in a looping maneuver over the top. In the slot, I shadowed the flight leader three hundred feet in trail over the top. As we passed through the inverted position at seven thousand feet, Wiz and Bob, the two wingmen, were equidistant from the Boss just as designed.

"Take it in," I radioed, the cue for both wingmen to add power to rendezvous in wing position on the back side of the loop. Off to my right, though, I could see Wiz was taking too much time.

"Keep it coming, Wiz," I said. We could still make it, but he needed to hurry up. Our four jets were now accelerating at four hundred knots. As we passed through vertical, nose down, the Boss increased his pull. Time was a'wasting.

Each second brought us closer to disaster.

I realized Wiz wasn't going to make it. I couldn't wait any longer for perfection. I gave the command to abort the rendezvous.

"Wiz, go clear."

"I can make it," he replied.

We were now just seven hundred feet away from hitting the surface of the Severn River. I couldn't squeeze an impromptu dialogue session into three more seconds before four A-4s splashed down and spoiled the festivities for one hundred thousand wide-eyed Naval graduates, family, and friends.

"GO CLEAR, WIZ!"

Wiz rolled slightly right and sharply pulled away to clear the formation. Without pausing, I slid rapidly into Wiz's vacant right wing position. Instead of four jets joined in Diamond formation, three of us came through the bottom at two hundred feet in a "Little V" configuration. No spectator, however, squinting up into the sunshine, could tell that the perfect air show had just slipped through the clouds.

We had worked hard to mask any shortcomings, so that few, if any, on the ground at Annapolis would know we had blown the "Fleur De Lis." In most people's minds, the Blue Angels could do no wrong. Yet those of us in the cockpit, with the yellow-striped ejection handle between our thighs just inches below and behind our right hands on the control stick, knew better. . . .

Fly like a bird

The air show over the Naval Air Station in Oceana, Virginia, home of the East Coast fighter and A-6 squadrons, during my first year on the team was a case in point. Just seconds into our steeply banked Diamond 360, at our lowest point only one hundred feet above the runway, I saw a blur go past the right side of my canopy. Hitting birds was not uncommon, and I was sure that Nordo, in the slot, had just swallowed a big one. I was wrong.

The next thing I knew, *my* engine started to rumble! A handful of feathers had just turned the Pratt and Whitney turbojet, its compressor blades turning at twelve thousand rpm, into a cement mixer. Immediately, I eased myself out of the formation, rolled the airplane wings level, and initiated a gentle climb toward our pre-briefed safe ejection area.

At one thousand feet, the engine was still running, but I knew I was in deep trouble. My instrument gauges looked like a Richter scale on steroids. I didn't touch the throttle.

"Oceana, Blue Angel three declaring emergency, need immediate landing, over."

In less than a minute, I had turned to a point where I could make the runway, *if* the engine kept running. The airplane vibrated. The landing gear dropped. Crash trucks lined the runway.

"Cleared to land Blue Angel three," called the tower. "Emergency equipment standing by."

I manipulated the flaps and speed brakes to adjust my speed on the approach, but I couldn't risk adjusting the throttle for fear the change in rpm would damage the engine even more. Yet, I didn't hesitate to pull the throttle to the shutoff position seconds later when rubber hit the runway. Braking the jet to a stop, I opened the canopy and unstrapped my safety harness. As the crash truck rolled to a stop next to the aircraft, I stood up in the cockpit and looked down the right intake of the Pratt and Whitney J52-P-408 turbojet engine. My jaw dropped. The compressor blades looked like shreds of aluminum foil. Goliath with a giant can opener couldn't have done more damage.

"Guess we've got a little engine problem," I said, with no waver in my voice.

"Had enough for the day?" replied the maintenance officer.

Before I climbed down, my helmet came off, and sunglasses and uniform hat went on.

My cool demeanor remained intact. That was the aviator's golden rule—better be dead than look bad. Whatever happened, act calm and be in control. Never show emotion in your voice. Always sound like Buck Rogers on the radio. "Yep, we got a little problem up here. Gonna have an emergency landing. Call the wife. Tell her to sell the house, and shoot the dog. Strong letter to follow."

The five remaining jets continued with the show above me, as if nothing had happened. In the thirty-five-year history of the Blue Angels, no air show had ever been cancelled due to an equipment failure. And that day was no exception.

It wasn't the first time with the Blues that I had been in a hurry to land.

During winter training five months earlier, we were in the middle of a four-plane practice session over the desert near El Centro. It was our first attempt at performing the Changeover Roll with four jets. The previous day's efforts with three planes had gone well, and we were enthused with our progress. The maneuver was one of our most demanding because, at the apex of the roll as our formation was rolling left through the inverted position, we would shift from a Right Echelon with three planes stacked down and aft on the Boss's right wing, to our trademark Diamond formation. If done right, the transformation from the crowd line perspective looked spectacular.

With wings level at two hundred feet off the ground and 350 knots, the Boss got us started with, "Smoke on. . . . Up we go." As we approached thirty degrees nose up, he called, "O . . . kay," and we stayed locked in position as he began a smooth roll to the left. Passing about twenty degrees left wing down, we began to slide toward a trail position, then individually made a move to our respective Diamond positions. Approaching inverted, Nordo called, "Compress it," and we added power to tighten the formation in Diamond position. I had executed the Changeover a dozen times already. I knew exactly what to do.

But this time I added too much power.

I knew I was in trouble the second before impact. My entire glare shield filled with airplanes as a sickening sound of ripping metal filled the sky. My jet seemed to tumble like a bowling pin, and the next thing I knew the plane was upside down, and pointed eighty degrees down at the mosaic of brown desert floor spinning below me. The airplane vibration jolted me back to reality.

I groped with my left hand for the ejection handle as I shoved the stick hard left. I desperately wanted to see if I could move the wings, get them underneath me, and roll the plane right side up.

I wanted to know if I could still fly.

I pulled the stick back slightly. The airplane righted itself. Ta-dah! At least I was sitting up. Then I got the nose up. I took my left hand away from the ejection controls. I looked out and could see the runway at El Centro forty miles in the distance, and started to make a beeline for the airstrip.

Nordo's radio transmission broke the silence. "Nag, are you okay?"

"So far," I said. "I'm setting up for a right base to an arrested landing."

Moments later in my rearview mirrors I could see the welcome sight of Nordo's jet sliding gently in toward me as we approached the outskirts of Brawley, three miles from the runway.

"Don't fly over town on your approach," he called.

"I'm in a bit of a hurry here, Nordo."

"Roger that, but you're about ready to lose part of your right wing."

The words were barely out of his mouth when I felt the aircraft shudder and begin to roll right as four feet of my right wing, including the right aileron, fell away.

In all my aviation training, I had never studied the feasibility of flying with only one aileron. If asked, I would have assumed that it was impossible. During the next few minutes, struggling to avoid Brawley, I learned the reality. With full cross stick and opposite rudder I managed to nurse the plane in for a landing. It wasn't pretty, but it was enough.

I joined with the three other planes, which landed on the adjacent runway, and the four of us taxied back to the ramp in our typical nose-to-tail formation, turned to chocks, and stopped. Once our crew chiefs saw the planes, their eyes got as big as pool balls. We shut down the engines, climbed out, walked back in formation, stopped, did an about-face, saluted, and shook hands. Only then did I allow myself to turn around and see the twisted metal of the first three jets.

At our debriefing fifteen minutes later, I could feel the sweat begin to bead up on my forehead. It started rolling down when it came time for each pilot to comment on any major safety item, and the flight leader, Denny Wisley, said, "From my cockpit, I didn't sense any unusual control movements that would have been cause for a problem. I *felt* some behind me."

Fred Stankovich, the right wingman, said, "Everything looked normal from my cockpit at the 'Compress it,' and the next thing I knew, the airplanes were just banging."

"Let me tell you what it looked like from *my* cockpit," I said. "It was ugly. I don't think that was the way it was designed to be flown." It was the understatement of the century. An hour and a half later, all of us confirmed my assessment, as we climbed back into the air using the spare aircraft and the two solo jets and flew the Changeover Roll seven or eight times.

News of the accident spread quickly throughout the network of Navy personnel and others who followed the Blues. Within minutes of landing, we called Bruce Davey back in Pensacola so that he could relay word to the families that we were okay. To assure Sonya, Bruce arrived on our front porch and gave her the good news, a reassuring gesture at a time when accurate news of our mishap, and comfort to a wife, was essential.

In eleven years of military flight, I had never as much as tapped a wing, much less lost part of one in mid-flight. In the flash of an eye, I had nearly killed the Boss and Stank, as well as myself. Combat had been harrowing at times, but with the Blues, the line between maximum performance and disaster had never seemed thinner. It humbled my pride and toughened my resolve. I still wanted to fly the perfect air show. It didn't occur to me that the travel schedule could be just as difficult.

Fueled by ambition, heated by Sterno

The Blue Angels' season from mid-March to mid-November was a seventy-thousand-mile, forty-five-city marathon. And we attacked it like a wind sprint.

The time clock for the week ended on Sunday night, when the Blues flew into Pensacola usually around sunset or later. After a short debriefing, I'd throw my blue flight bag and suitcase into the Porsche and drive home. If I didn't dilly-dally around with the coming week's schedule or administrative items, I could make it home by 8:30 P.M. My weekly schedule was uncomplicated. Eight hours later, I woke up and began paying homage once more to the elite assignment I lived and breathed in my life as a Blue Angel.

Everything I did was focused on preparing for the next air show. Monday was for laundering flight suits, shining boots, checking mail, and paying bills. Tuesday meant a squadron meeting, a practice show, and paperwork. Ditto Wednesday. Thursday, I was out the door and in the cockpit by nine o'clock, bound for Chicago, Miami, San Diego, wherever our schedule told us to go. We would fly direct to the air show site, orbit for fifteen minutes to confirm our visual check points and flight lines, then set up for the first of our six arrival maneuvers to prepare for the following day's practice show.

Occasionally, we'd break the routine. Bruce Davey had left the

Navy after his tour with the Blues and was spending time with his folks at their home in McCall, Idaho. On our trip to the Pacific Northwest, we decided to make a special appearance over Payette Lake in Squire's honor just prior to our refueling stop at Mountain Home Air Force Base. En route to Idaho, we established radio contact with Bruce and gave him a heads-up on our arrival time. Fuel was getting low, but we elected to continue because we knew he had assembled every man, woman, child, dog, and cat in the entire McCall region for our fly-by, and we didn't want to make them wait.

The sight and sound must have been spectacular as we roared across the lake at tree top level, smoke pouring out all six exhausts. Squire was ecstatic, but we were gasping. Our fuel gauges were indicating as low as our altimeters. No one on the team prayed, so the only responsible thing to do was complete a high-performance climb to fifteen thousand feet, reduce the power to near idle, and coast into Mountain Home—on fumes.

Friday during air show week gave us an opportunity to visit schools, hospitals, and television stations. After a fast-food lunch on our way to the airfield, we faced a forest of reporters' microphones, and autographs for the elderly, disabled, and children who were bussed in to watch us fly the practice show.

All of it was a prelude to the Main Event. From the moment we awoke on Saturday morning, the Blue Angels were on automatic pilot.

Exercise and breakfast by 9:00 A.M.

Suntanning and shoes spit-shined by noon.

Police motorcade from the hotel to the field by 1:00 P.M.

In the briefing room by 1:15 P.M.

Walk down to the jets at 2:30 P.M.

Strapped in the cockpit at 2:33 P.M.

Taxiing to the runway at 2:40 P.M.

Takeoff at the beginning of our FAA waiver time at 2:45 P.M. sharp.

After landing and a quick maintenance update for the ground crew, we had another thirty minutes for autograph signing and handshakes. Then it was an hour-long debrief before going back to the hotel room and a hot shower then racing off to a community reception.

Sunday's show was similar, except that thirty minutes after debriefing, we were back on the runway, working stick and throttle, bound for Pensacola.

Each air show generated a series of non-stop expectations, from sit-down dinners to stand-up remarks. My evening "commitment" attire of gray slacks and blue blazer became just as predictable. I got so tired of saying, "Hi, my name's Jim Horsley," I thought of breaking with tradition by launching into a handshake with, "You don't know me, but I'm 'Hello My Name Is.'" At receptions, I lived on a diet of Gulf shrimp, Brie cheese spread, and club soda. I swallowed so many Hawaiian meatballs, I was convinced at least half of all America's fine hotels were heated by Sterno.

In these fourteen-hour days, I sometimes wondered why I didn't malfunction more often than the airplanes. On the evening following our Saturday Chicago show, my jet was flyable, but not in formation because of a stability augmentation problem. But we had a second show the next day. Since the Blue Angels didn't offer rain checks, I flew back to Pensacola late that night in the wounded jet, arrived at 11:00 P.M., gulped some hot coffee, jumped in our spare airplane, and arrived back in Chicago at 2:00 A.M. The maintenance crew worked through dark and dawn to get the plane ready, including painting a new number "4" on the tail. That was the Blue Angel way, applying a clean, fresh, glossy exterior to a high-performance machine.

I kept living on seven hours sleep, never stopping, and never quite totally satisfied with my own performance or the team's. Ambition begat pride, which begat needing to be perfect, which begat working smarter, faster, longer. Which begat more ambition. What fueled this cycle was my own high-octane determination made up of one part caffeine, two parts testosterone, and three parts will that almost ran me to ruin.

During my first year, the evening prior to our departure to Philadelphia, my appendix nearly ruptured. Within hours I was whisked into surgery. I missed three weekends with the team. When I finally got back in the cockpit (ignoring a doctor's advice to not overdo), I really had to scramble to regain the concentration and focus that had dissipated by not flying for nineteen days. I couldn't be bothered with human limitations. I had a career to fly. Sometimes the only thing that could get my attention was a good laugh.

Gambling on gravel

We flew our A-4 Skyhawks to each air show site, and whether heading beyond the Rockies, or grazing over the Midwest farm belt at twenty-five thousand feet, it wasn't uncommon to share the skies with a commercial airliner. When radio communications from the FAA control centers indicated we were approaching visual range, the Boss would radio the plane's captain.

"United, Blue Angels at your one o'clock ten miles slightly high."

The real fun started when we closed to within eight miles. At the flight leader's command "Spread it. . . . Rolling in," all six airplanes would simultaneously flip upside down, and then tighten up the formation. Just for decoration, we turned on the smoke. Our flight leader would radio the airliner's captain: "Check your two o'clock. Care to join us?"

The captain, in turn, would ask his passengers the same question. Though I couldn't see their reactions, I could hear the unison "click" of dozens of seat belts as one half the plane moved to the other side of the plane to see our impromptu stunt. The sight of six Blue Angels flying upside down, safely out of range yet within full view, had to be a better value than the liveliest in-flight movie.

I never thought that taking off would be a challenge, until we flew to Nevada for the Reno Air Races and Air Show. At night, all the stars were out, including the Gatlin Brothers and country singer Roy Clark. During the day, the Blue Angels were the hot ticket, as ABC sports prepared to film our presentation for *Wide World Of Sports*. There was just one problem; the runway wasn't wide enough for our four-plane Diamond takeoff. On the morning of the air show, before the crowd arrived, we needed to know if the number four plane and its pilot, Jim Horsley, could take off alongside his teammates—in the gravel.

We subjected our opinion to scientific testing. I got behind the wheel of the crew truck to check the ruts, floored the gas pedal, and hung on. I was satisfied that none of the million rocks in my wake would prevent me from retracting the plane's landing gear. However, the brown cloud that billowed out the back of the crew truck was nothing compared to what happened six hours later when I pushed the A-4 to full power.

It was like driving a '51 Chevy pickup. I half expected to see a Nevada State Trooper pull me over. The video replay was one for the highlight reel.

Sometimes, the outrageous happened away from the planes. The day of our show in St. Petersburg, Florida, I was dressed in a canary yellow flight suit, on my way out the hotel door. Sonya, who had joined me for the weekend, said, "You can't go out looking like that." Granted, the bright Tweety Bird yellow apparel was not the team's garment of choice (we threatened to burn them at the end of the season).

"What are you talking about?" I asked her.

She pointed at the flight suit. "Your blue shorts! You can see them right through the flight suit."

I checked the mirror. She was right. Unfortunately, I didn't have any other color. Off they came. Minutes later, preoccupied by getting ready for the air show, I forgot about it—at least until the autograph line following our landing. I was signing brochures and answering questions from the crowd, when a woman in a straw hat and sunglasses stepped up and shouted, "Hey hotshot, what do you wear beneath that flight suit?"

Stuttering, I began to embarrassingly reply, "It's ah, ah, not anything that. . . ." I then recognized the wife of another Blue Angel whom Sonya had included in the joke.

I wish I'd included Sonya in more of our trips. I might have rediscovered what it was like to have a real marriage. I might have done something outrageous like hold her hand, or forget about the Blue Angels long enough to see a movie or walk on the beach. Had Sonya and I had more of those moments, I might have understood why our marriage was slowly unraveling. Because I would have seen the frayed ends that were all around me.

Romantic candlelight — and silence

I could have blamed the Blue Angels. The hurry-up demands of our air show schedule allowed me only one full week at home in ten months. I could count the number of family meals we enjoyed together each month on one hand. It was rare that I cleared my schedule when I was home so that Sonya and I could enjoy an evening out with just each other. As Jeff and Shannon got settled into carpools and school, Sonya took a part-time job selling cosmetics at the military exchange. I encouraged her. I didn't expect her to stay home and keep polishing the stove. In fact, I wished she could have packed her bags and joined me, because the gregarious, loving side of me wanted her to experience this elite fraternity known as the Blue Angels. And so I tried.

When we got to the hotel lobby that weekend in St. Petersburg, I learned, to my chagrin, that there was nothing set up for wives or the families. The only recreational or social opportunities with any hint of ambience were an indoor pool with plastic lounge chairs and the hospitality hour that evening. I tried to graciously introduce Sonya as my wife. While she looked beautiful and poised, 95 percent of all eye contact and conversation was focused on me.

It felt flattering and terribly awkward. No one talked to Sonya. It was as if she were invisible. She was wise and saw through others' clumsy social etiquette. Those who tried to be polite said, "And you're Jim's wife. How nice to meet you." Smile. They would give her a little-squeeze handshake, offer a refill of gin and tonic, and then quickly go back to quizzing me about the Blues. I could feel Sonya chafing inside. When women introduced themselves, her antennae were up. She knew what they were interested in. And so did I.

Most of the time Sonya stayed home. Whether I headed out for another air show, or whether I came home, I felt the distance between us begin to widen. There were two types of homecomings. After landing at the base on Sunday night, the six of us would jump in our cars, drive home, pick up the wives, and race to Trader Jon's Tavern, a legendary gathering place for aviators in Pensacola. And it had to be a race. Sticking to the thirty-five mile-per-hour speed limit along Barancas Boulevard didn't exist. We had to race. I had to be no less than two feet off Mike Nord's bumper. From the front seat of my Porsche 924 I had to be able to read the expiration month on his license tab. I had to go fast. I had to push the envelope.

Sonya got fed up. "Do we have to do this? Didn't you do enough racing during the week? Can't we just drive to dinner?"

I didn't pay much attention. I didn't think about any other way to live. Whether I had an airplane throttle, a steering wheel, or a bar glass in my hand, I wanted to go fast and hard, and hope my wife enjoyed the ride.

The second kind of homecoming was strangely subdued. On other Sundays, when the Blues boomed home, I set the Porsche on automatic pilot, zipped in the driveway, and staggered in the front door.

I'd set down my flight bag and give Sonya a peck on the cheek. She was the picture of consistency. She always gave me a warm hug. She always had a candlelit dinner ready. She was always ready to spend a few precious moments with me. I should have considered myself one of the luckiest men alive (if not one of the most tired). After a week of practice flights, hospitality receptions, press interviews, air shows, autograph signings, and crowds, I was out of breath and out of words. If I managed to say ten words to Sonya between salad and dessert, then it was a major address.

I'd mention the size of the air show crowd.

"The only crowds I experienced this week," Sonya once replied, "were at the kids' doctor's office and the grocery store."

When I didn't respond, it was because I hadn't bothered to listen to the woman who had worked so hard to welcome me home. If I had looked up from my plate, I would have seen what my wife's eyes were saying to me. If I had just taken the time to ask what was going on in her life, I would have seen that her eyes were moist. Then, I may have seen her dimples I used to delight in whenever she smiled.

Why didn't I notice? A few years later, we were watching a television special on the twentieth anniversary of the manned moon landing. One of the astronauts said, "When we got to the moon, we recognized the degree of perfection it took to get us there. When we looked back at earth, everything looked perfect as well. And when we came back from the moon, we expected all of life to be that way."

The astronaut looked over at his wife. Immediately, I could see in her face the pain she endured during his years of work. I looked over at Sonya and saw the same look of frustration and emptiness.

The Blue Angels experience was my pinnacle and my passion. I was consumed by the demands, the exhilaration, the pursuit of perfection. Making it to the top gave me license to say, "I've trained for this. I've earned this. I'm enjoying this." The opportunity was so rare, the reward so sweet, that I never stopped to consider what was happening to my wife, to my children. And most of all, to me.

The perfect day to be alone

On an early August afternoon, Seattle's Lake Washington and Mt. Rainier shimmered in the sun. It was time for Seafair, the city's weeklong summer fest capped off by the traditional Sunday hydroplane races. Prior to the day's championship final, half a million spectators enjoyed our forty-minute thrill overhead. Of the nearly eighty air shows we performed that season, this one was, perhaps, the most special.

For once I was back home in the Northwest.

And for once, the forty-minute demonstration routine we had poured ourselves into was flawless. As close to perfection as I could ever hope to fly. I felt confident beyond words as our six jets made one final low-altitude fly-by over Lake Washington. That evening, at the VIP reception, I basked in the adulation of

The author, Jim Horsley, age two, and his father in Soda Springs, Idaho, 1948.

Sonya pins Jim with his Navy Wings of Gold, in Pensacola, Florida, fall, 1970.

Sonya Horsley kisses son Jeff on the eve of his dad's departure to Vietnam, 1972.

VA-115 squadron aboard the USS Midway *during the Vietnam War, early 1972. Jim Horsley is standing in the top row, third from the right. Close friends Mike McCormick (second row from the top, third from the right) and Arlo Clark (third row from the top, fourth from the right) were the last two A-6 pilots to die in Vietnam.*

Father and son are reunited after Jim comes home from Vietnam, spring, 1973.

An A-6 launches from the flight deck of the USS Midway, *"headed to North Vietnam, and loaded for bear," 1972. Photo by Tom Watson.*

The 1981 Blue Angel flight team (left to right) Lieutenant Bud Hunsaker, USN; Lieutenant Commander Stu Powrie, USN; Lieutenant Commander Jim Horsley, USN; Major Tim Dineen, USMC; Commander Denny Wisley, USN; Lieutenant Commander Bob Stephens, USN; Lieutenant Commander Jack Ekl, USN; Lieutenant Commander Kevin Miller, USN.

Manning up for an early morning pre-show flight.

"Best seat in the house"—the view from "the slot" position on the back side of the Diamond Loop. Photo by Harry Gann.

Don't flinch. The Blue Angels in their Echelon Parade formation. Photo by Harry Gann.

The Blue Angels streak across the sky, thirty-six inches from wingtip to canopy, in their Diamond formation.

Jim Horsley and fellow pilot Mike Nord (right) celebrate at the Blue Angels' 1980 season-ending party.

The Horsley family roundup includes Jim, Jeff, Sonya, and Shannon, 1996.

Jim and his mother, 1988.

"Marital bliss . . . or else!"

Tonya and Tad Clark at a dedication ceremony for Arlo, 1993.

Jim returns to the Gia Lam railroad yard in Hanoi, nearly twenty years after his 1972 bombing run.

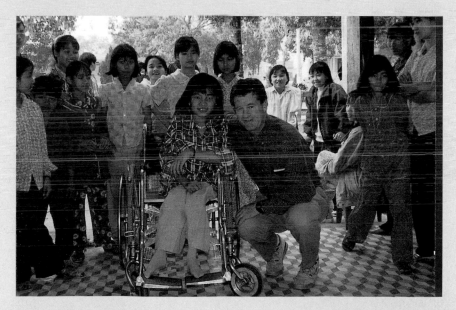

The author with his friend, Thui, at the Thuy Au Orphanage outside of Hanoi, 1997.

Jim Horsley with World Vision President Bob Seiple (middle) and buddy Dave Dornsife in Bangkok, Thailand, 1991.

"Hope" Petronella, a Romanian angel of joy, with Sonya, Jim, and daughter Shannon, 1992.

being celebrated as one of the finest military pilots in the world. I had achieved more than I'd ever imagined.

Two hours later, the champagne bottles were dry, the hors d'oeuvres were gone, and I was walking down the hall to my room at the city's Edgewater Hotel. I opened the door, walked inside, and clicked the dead bolt closed. All the room lights were off.

I stretched out facedown on the carpet.

I felt so depleted, so tired, and so terribly empty.

Why, after I had accomplished so much—flown so far, so high, so fast—did I feel such a deep inner groaning?

Why did I feel so unhappy?

I had two months to go with the Blue Angels. I had no idea what I would do for an encore.

Something felt terribly wrong. Yet I wasn't sure I had the courage to face it.

6

The High Cost of Living

"Come now, let us reason together," says the LORD.
"Though your sins are like scarlet, they shall be as white as snow. . . ."

—ISAIAH 1:18

The desperate emptiness I felt at the Edgewater was as subtle as an air-raid siren. The alarm had sounded, but I didn't know where to reach, or how to turn it off. So, I went with my strength. I kept it all inside. I sucked it up. I made sure I kept on going as if nothing had changed.

The next morning I joined the other Blues for an early breakfast, a briefing, and a fast flight out of town. There wasn't any time to stop and assess what was ticking inside me. I still had a career to catch, and I didn't want to be late.

My final three months as a Blue Angel wearied me to the bone. I was out of gas, physically and emotionally. Everyone on the team was worn down. Nerves were short. So were tempers. After nine months of flying around (including all the hours we spent in the air), I felt like I flew the final twenty-five air shows with Bob Greaves sitting in the back yelling, "Keep going! Keep going!"

The finish line came in Pensacola on November 15. When we rolled those six jets down the runway in a six-point Delta landing for the last time, I was relieved and wistful.

It was over. My dream had landed. Over 150 air shows and no maintenance cancellations, three times as many practices, and no one hurt. The legacy of prior teams had been preserved, and I'd passed the test. My earlier doubts had been answered, and I had experienced the ultimate in high-performance flight demonstration.

The season-ending party that night was a deserving toast to having done our jobs and done them superbly.

"Let's raise one to Horsley's damaged right wing!" said the narrator, a prodding reference to my bump-and-run maneuver over El Centro a year earlier.

I, however, had the last laugh.

"That wing will never fly again, gentlemen," I said. "It's being retired. Besides, I've got a one-of-a kind reminder of my mid-air nudge with the Boss and Stank." On the jagged blue and yellow metal fragment, Nordo had scribbled, "I've never seen two friends closer in my life." Stank added, "A closer friend could not be found."

At our official party two weeks later, I presented going-away gifts to my three crew chiefs, Keith Hulbert, Bill Barber, and Bill Weakley. For the past year, each man had worked to ensure that my jet had been thoroughly prepared for every flight. Keith gave me a nice set of pewter beer mugs and a serving platter. Barber and Weakley handed me a nicely wrapped gift box. I opened it up and there, lounging under a layer of tissue paper, was a King James Bible.

"Thanks guys, that's very thoughtful of you," I said.

Quietly, I was embarrassed. Here we were, at a boisterous farewell party with some of the most testosterone-driven men in the military, and they give me a Bible! To be polite, I nervously thumbed open to the inside front cover and saw a handwritten note: "What one must do to enter heaven." And then, following their references to eight different verses, were the words, "Now read the book of 1 John to learn how God wants us to live."

I shook their hands, handed Sonya the Bible, and tossed down another gin and tonic. Then I turned and said good-bye to the two most demanding, rewarding years of my life.

I was satisfied with what I had accomplished as a member of one of the world's most elite and revered flying fraternities. And I was ready to move on. I no longer envied going to work at 450 knots and looking up into the armpit of a Navy jet. I wanted to build a life beyond the Blue Angels. I wanted to grab the next brass ring.

I had already been on the phone to my new boss. The job was all set. I would soon begin a new career in a new city, two thousand miles west of Pensacola. While Sonya stayed behind with Judy Ekl before flying out west, I would drive the two kids and our two Lhasa Apso dogs. As I hugged the neighbors, our oldest dog, Gomer, collapsed on the sidewalk. Sonya had overdosed the tranquilizer pills that were supposed to help quiet the dog (and ensure my peace of mind) for the four-day trek ahead. Gomer finally lifted his head, and his glazed eyes pleaded with us to just let him sleep it off. We obliged, leaving Pensacola and thirteen years of naval aviation in the rearview mirror.

High interest in business

My new civilian suits felt about as stiff as my new business cards:

> James B. Horsley
> Development Director
> Bedford Properties, Lafayette, California

Though I was a stranger to commercial real estate, I savored the challenge. Within months I was overseeing the company's struggling industrial park and shopping center projects in Portland. It didn't take long for me to compile a marketing study that convinced my bosses that their investments were about to take a nosedive, just like the dog.

The owner took note. He liked my ideas and aggressiveness. After only a few months in the San Francisco Bay area, I sensed a change coming when Peter Bedford asked me if I would be willing to open a regional office in Portland. Before he could say, "Oregon," I asked, "How soon can I pack?"

The relocation was like moving to Camelot. Our castle was a thirty-four-hundred-square-foot home in Lake Oswego, an upscale suburb south of Portland. Completely redecorated, the home had a downstairs office with a fireplace that looked out onto a grassy lawn, and a private boathouse on Blue Heron Bay. Sonya strolled from room to room and kept pinching herself. For at least an hour or two, I forgot about work.

Summer nights offered instant entertainment. The recipe was simple: Just add water. One Friday evening, Sonya and I were enjoying the sunset on our deck with Judy Ekl, who had come out to visit from Pensacola feeling the reverberations of a divorce from her husband, Jack. Some friends pulled up in their run-about. "Hey, how about joining us for dinner at a waterfront restaurant on the far end of Blue Heron Bay?"

"We've got dinner going," I said. "What if we catch up with you a little bit later?"

"Later" turned out to be about 11:00 P.M., after the three of us had done major damage to a bottle of Tanqueray Gin. I decided it was time for a boat ride. I fired up the engine, backed out of the boathouse, and Sonya, Judy, and I began tooling across the water. It was pitch black outside. After clearing the lagoon, I jammed the throttle all the way open until we were going twice the speed of reason. Then, to ensure maximum enjoyment, I turned off the running lights and stood up in the boat.

Two things caught my eye. One was the moonlight shimmering off the water. The other was the red flashing lights of the police boat that pulled up next to mine. I didn't panic. I knew exactly what to say.

"Officer, we were just tooling on down to a party. Care to join us?"

To my amazement, he said, "Might catch you later!"

During daylight hours, I worked as hard as I played. I had to. Interest rates hovered at 21 percent. It was not the golden age of commercial real estate. In fact, the entire economic climate felt like a nuclear winter. My job was to save two major shopping centers that had as many "For Lease" signs as tenants. I also had to kick-start the expansion of a fifty-four-acre industrial park. Every morning I pulled up to one of our shopping centers and learned of yet another bankruptcy. I felt like the living antithesis to Ed McMahon; instead of delivering checks to winners of the Publishers Clearing House Sweepstakes, I was *looking* for money. Tenants saw me coming and ran. They were packing up and leaving so fast I began to get windburn from their doors closing behind them.

Thank goodness the Christmas holiday season arrived. Business was so dead at the Holly Farm retail mall, I offered local craft vendors free rent so they could sell their wares—anything to get people to come to the shopping center. To help make the promotion a success, I arranged for a helicopter to fly in Santa Claus. While Santa filled up the front seat next to the pilot, I wedged in the back. I had flown scores of combat missions and Blue Angel air shows, but I was never more terrified than that day, as I looked down below and saw a sea of children surging against the restraining lines while the chopper prepared to set down on their tiny, little heads.

The ride continued to be rough. In my vow to be successful, I worked eighteen-hour days. I became married to the phone. Meals with Sonya and the kids became extinct. I computed spreadsheets and rent options into the wee hours of the morning. It must have been half past moon one night when I came to bed. Sonya asked, "How long are you going to stay at this thing?"

I lowered myself onto the mattress.

"Until my body gives out."

What did I know.

Driving lessons

My prophecy was fulfilled a few weeks later on a Saturday afternoon at a local health club. I had been shooting basketballs with two college guys, when I began to say to myself, "I can beat them without breaking a sweat."

I threw out the invitation. "How about a game of Cutthroat? It's all against one, one against all, each man for himself." I stood there and grinned. These two young lions looked at me and saw lunch.

For the first few minutes, I was all flash. A couple of moves even surprised me. Then the competition swooped in. They played with me like a VCR. ("There's Horsley driving to the basket in slow motion. There's his wiry opponent faking one way, then driving past him the other way in fast-forward. Basket good . . . again!")

My lungs were beginning to tire. "Give me the ball," I said. I took the leather, lowered my head, and drove for the hoop. I told my thirty-six-year-old legs to move, but they refused to get the message.

Then, something popped. It felt like someone had hit the back of my right leg with a baseball bat. I crumpled up in a pile. My shoulder hit the court first, then my hip. I twisted over and reached for the back of my ankle. There wasn't a trace of muscle, cord, or sinew between my heel and my calf, which was beginning to pound like a tom-tom. I had played enough gym ball to know that the game was over. I had severed my Achilles tendon.

It was ugly. I wanted to scream, but my bravado wouldn't let me. ("Keep it in. Hold onto the pain. Don't let them know you're in trouble.") Onlookers wanted to help me, but I refused. Somehow, I managed to stand up, limp to my four-speed Honda Accord, and drive to the hospital, where I crawled from the car through the parking lot on my hands and knees. The automatic door to the emergency room swung open when my right hand hit the mat.

The prognosis was immediate: a complete tear. The doctor wrapped my leg, offered me a pair of crutches, and directed Sonya to take me home.

"Keep him warm. I want you back at eight o'clock tomorrow morning for surgery. No drinking after midnight." I made sure I followed doctor's orders. After polishing off several margaritas that night at a dinner party, I carefully checked my watch, and at one minute to midnight, I gave Sonya my glass.

The day after surgery I came home in a full leg cast. A severed Achilles tendon, I was told, usually took three months to heal. I knew that was too long to wait. Morning commutes became a new Olympic event. Every day was a new time trial. I mastered the "Straight Leg Lift and Hoist" by opening the door of the company station wagon and literally swinging my right leg into the front seat until it veered diagonally from my hip socket at a forty-five-degree angle, stretched across the passenger seat. While driving, I pumped the gas and brake pedals with my left foot until my left thigh became as hard as a frozen holiday ham.

Indoors, I tried not to "push the envelope" as much as usual. I didn't always succeed. One evening while working alone at the office, I got up from my chair and hobbled over to the printer. Everything cooperated except the cast's tiny protective rubber heel. It caught the plastic protective floor mat. Two-thirds of me went sprawling under the desk. My twenty-pound plaster of Paris leg jutted up in the air. I didn't know whether to salute it, or curse it. I winced and wiggled for a good ten minutes. Unfortunately I couldn't reach the phone, otherwise I would have dialed one of two numbers: 9-1-1, or 1-800-GET-A-LIFE.

I was beginning to see a pattern. First, the economy collapses. Then *collapse.* The final blow came on Mother's Day. Though brunch hadn't been on the agenda, I convinced the family I could brave the crowds. With Sonya driving and me in the backseat, barking directions, we hunted for restaurants. Finally, we found a place whose line didn't snake out to the parking lot.

Sonya stopped the car, and I gave Jeff his orders. "Don't stand in line. Just walk up and ask how long we'd have to wait." Being a self-conscious thirteen-year-old, Jeff didn't want to be seen. He shuffled toward the front door and peeked inside the restaurant. I couldn't believe it. While I loved the kids, I didn't have the capacity, at that moment, to silence my frustration.

I threw open the door and swung my cast to the ground. Then, I grabbed my crutches and threw them onto the parking lot.

"Do I have to take care of this too?" I bellowed.

"Jim, get back in the car!" shrieked Sonya.

"Not a chance," I huffed.

Right about then, Jeff came running back to announce that everything in the restaurant was full. It didn't matter. My furor had just created one vacancy in the front seat.

"Okay, let's try somewhere else," I snapped.

"I'm not going anywhere with you. I just want to go home," yelled Sonya. Home to Camelot, where our storybook life was beginning to dim.

Total net loss

When my cast came off, the reattached Achilles tendon was still a long way from being 100 percent. And I had some other nagging pains. The list included an inflamed temper, a growing intolerance for people and situations that bordered on rudeness, an inability to sit still, and an insatiable need to win.

I wasn't healthy to be around. Often, I would ask the kids if they wanted to go to the store with me. Every time we got in the car, however, I ended up driving by a piece of property I was eyeing for a new real estate deal.

"This will only take a minute," I promised. An hour later we would pull up to the grocery store. After a while, Jeff and Shannon refused to go anywhere with me. By choosing work over family, I felt more and more anxious about both.

The most uneasy and frustrated person of all, however, was Sonya. She had learned to ride out the fearful, lonely years of being the wife of a Navy pilot. Moving to Lake Oswego and reuniting with high school and college friends had delighted her. I would be able to shelve the long hours, come home at a normal hour, and eat pot roast that didn't need to be warmed up.

I wanted that too. I wanted a job that didn't suck the life out of me, but the job kept winning out. I couldn't seem to slow down. And I could see the resentment in Sonya building. It was all in her body language and eyes, a look that said, "He's not listening," or "He's not really here," or "Who is this person I married?"

We had lost something along the way, but neither of us could put a finger on it. And we couldn't talk about what was wrong, because we didn't know how to communicate without increasing the tension. We knew we wanted something more, but we couldn't seem to find it at home. As a spontaneous attempt to improve the state of our marriage, we decided to get away for a weekend at a cozy beachfront condominium on the Oregon coast, courtesy of some thoughtful friends.

The setting was gorgeous. On Saturday, the sun came out and we played tennis. Though neither of us was very good, we tried to relax. That evening, we were sitting on the couch, trying to get used to the company of the pounding surf, a roaring fireplace, and each other. Sonya got up and walked into the kitchen to fix a snack.

Moments later I heard her shriek. I jumped up. Immediately, I pictured a kitchen knife and a cut finger. I jumped up and went to the kitchen There, I saw Sonya standing over the sink. Her hands shaking.

"What's wrong?" I asked.

Sonya stared at her hand and cried.

"It's gone! My diamond! It's gone!"

I looked at the gold band on her left hand. It was bare.

I knew she was devastated, and I didn't want to add to her misery. I wanted to make it better. "Don't worry, we'll find it. It's not that serious," I said. "It's just a diamond." I put my arms around her, and we stood at the sink. I had never seen my wife cry so deeply.

I rescued some Kleenex, Sonya dried her eyes, and we started searching all over the apartment for the diamond. We looked in the garbage disposal, on the floor, under the furniture. We crawled on our knees and felt along every baseboard. All we found was a paperclip and two dimes.

Sonya stayed up half the night in tears. The next morning, we dressed and headed for the beach. At Sonya's suggestion, we took a short detour and walked down to the tennis court where we had been playing the day earlier. It had rained all night. The court was covered with puddles and dead, brown leaves. I walked near the bench where we had been stretching, wondering where her diamond could have possibly gone.

I stood on the tennis court with my hands in my pockets. I

knew it wasn't just a diamond. To Sonya, it was a symbol of our marriage, the only thing she had left that represented the hope and promise of a relationship that had dulled with time. And now that hope was gone.

The sun peeked through the thick, gray clouds and covered the court. I looked around. As Sonya walked over near the baseline, I saw something catch her eye. Something on the court. It was either a coin or the sun's glare off the rainwater. She looked closer and bent down. It wasn't a coin. It was something tinier, shining brilliantly.

I froze.

"I can't believe it!" said Sonya. "Here it is! What are the odds of this? What a gift from God!"

I raced over to see for myself.

She had found her diamond.

The mistake of going to church

When we got back home to Lake Oswego, I took Sonya's diamond to a local jeweler, who secured it on her slender gold band in about an hour. When I picked up the ring, I thanked him, and I felt like asking, "Do you also repair lives that have become unglued?" So many things in my life—my marriage, my career, and my relationship with Jeff and Shannon—seemed unstable. I had always believed I could do anything. Now, I wasn't so sure.

I thought I could move from my success with the Blue Angels and replicate my achievements in a brand-new career. Reality had flown in my face. When people learned what I had done in an airplane, they expected me to perform similar miracles in a depressed real estate market. The last thing I wanted was to earn a reputation for being unsuccessful—which, in my mind, was exactly what was happening.

The absolute low point came during an overnight business trip to California. After a late dinner I went back to the hotel. Once inside my room, I became uneasy. I didn't like the person I saw pacing in front of the hallway mirror. To me, his life was a contradiction.

I couldn't escape the growing unease I felt between my public bravado and my private despair. I didn't dare lift up the protective visor and let others see the things I could barely admit to myself: that deep inside, I was hurting.

That things weren't working out quite the way I had hoped.

And that in the constant push to excel and look good, I felt more and more empty and alone. The flat-line emotions and mental exhaustion I'd felt on the floor of the Edgewater Hotel had resurfaced. Only one piece of the landscape had changed. In Lake Oswego, Sonya started attending the Mountain Park Baptist Church with the kids. Reluctantly, I followed them. One Sunday, she made the mistake of writing our name and phone number on a pew pad. A few days later, I received a call from a guy wanting me to attend a men's retreat at the Cannon Beach Christian Conference Center on the Oregon coast. I said no.

The problem was I never should have gone to church, especially in my weakened condition. Otherwise, I never would have found myself leaning forward on Sundays as the pastor began telling stories of real people whose lives had been changed by a real God. It wasn't so much his message but his personal warmth that spoke to me.

I started to gravitate toward Sundays much the same way I had looked forward to spending time with my high school Young Life club leaders, Jerry and Delores Franz, who had opened their home and their hearts to high school students in Billings. Through skits, laughter, and good discussions, we talked about faith and a God who loved people unconditionally. A summer camp in Colorado spurred my interest, but when I left home for college, it didn't seem relevant.

Now, almost twenty years later, some of my earlier interest in spiritual things was returning. And the church had gotten wind of it.

After I got back from my business trip to California, I called the church and asked if there was still room for me to go on the retreat. There was. I squeezed into the last remaining car right next to the pastor, Bob Westgate. As the trip unfolded, I knew I was a living contradiction:

While I respected him, I squirmed the whole ride.

When he prayed over dinner at a restaurant, I prayed he would stop.

When we broke up into small discussion groups the next morning, I dreaded opening the Bible, even though I brought my own brand-new unopened version that I had received from my crew chiefs.

When our small group leader said, "Turn to John," I turned to the guy next to me whose real name was Pete. Though I tried not to draw attention to myself, I ended up startling half the group when I pried open the Bible's previously untouched gold-leaf edge pages, which sounded like a small hurricane rustle of dead leaves.

I didn't say much to the other men. However, from their first "hellos" they accepted me, no questions asked. I didn't feel judged. I felt welcomed and affirmed. It was as if they were related to the Franzes. After twenty years, a bit of the warmth I had forgotten started to come back.

That afternoon I walked on the beach. I walked until I felt as alone as I had ever been. I thought about where I had been, and what I had done in life. I pondered the hurtfulness, and the hardness that had crowded into my existence. I hadn't been that way in the six years of Sunday school in Soda Springs. I hadn't behaved that way at Young Life back in Billings. I wasn't the same man that Sonya thought she'd married as a bright-eyed college student.

My dream of successful, well-off, and well-liked had become

one continuous long night of restlessness. On the beach, I began to understand why. My Blue Angel persona masked the lack of character and values that was destroying my marriage. I had failed myself, I had failed my family, and I had failed the God of my youth.

My pursuit of fame had perjured my soul, and my yearning for recognition was a futile attempt to ignore the shame that came with the pain I'd caused others. The sporadic attendance at Christmas and Easter services seemed hollow and hypocritical. At what point had I sacrificed all that had meaning, and chosen a path that had fed the lie?

When I got back to my room, I closed the door and sat on the bed.

And I began to weep.

At the evening meeting that night, a number of men stood up and talked about the reality of God in each of their lives. I sat and listened. All I could hear was the truth of my failure in the things that should have mattered.

I couldn't dance around this anymore.

I knew too much.

I couldn't escape the transgressions of my past.

I had gained elite status with the Blues. I had become one of the best in the world at what I wanted to be—and experienced a victory without substance. The Jesus in my Bible achieved no status, yet had claimed the ultimate victory.

Would I trade my present for His future? Either God was going to be real in my life, or He was not. If He is real, I thought, then I had better find a way to make Him real in my life, right now. Late that night, in the darkness of my room, I prayed for His forgiveness and mercy, for His acceptance and grace.

The next night over dinner at home, I told Sonya what had happened. I decided to lift the visor just a crack. "I'm not sure what this all means, but over the weekend I made a firm decision that I've got to be serious about my relationship with God and rely on the promise of Jesus to offer new life. I don't know where it will lead, but it's got to be better than where I've been."

Then I paused for a moment.

"I do know that I need to ask for your continued forgiveness for everything I've put you and the kids through." She didn't need a clarification. She knew I wasn't talking about temper tantrums on Mother's Day.

A month following my tour with the Blue Angels, we had encountered the most painful day of our sixteen years of marriage. The kids played nearby as we sat in the park in Walnut Creek and confronted Sonya's worst fears. She sobbed in anguish as she tried to comprehend the reality of my involvement with other women during my time with the Blues. I had ripped away her self-esteem and trust by violating my marriage commitment. And there was nothing I could say to take away her pain. We somehow managed to stay together over the next weeks and months, but her wounds would take years to heal.

Now, two years later, as we sat in the kitchen, I told her, "I know I've left some permanent marks on the chalkboard, but as of tonight I want to believe we can begin to start over with a clean slate. I want to pray and commit to you that we can move forward with a marriage that can be more of what you anticipated when you married me."

Life— that week, that month, that next year—was not perfect by any means. But gradually, Sonya began to sense a change, and we found reasons to celebrate what we still meant to each other.

Four years later, on December 21, 1988, my greatest challenge was how to spend our twentieth anniversary. I could let go of being a Blue Angel. My marriage, however, was something I wanted to hold on to, forever. I wanted to renew our wedding vows, and I wanted it to be a surprise.

It was. Jeff and Shannon stood at my side as a fire crackled in the fireplace. When the harpist began playing the wedding march, I looked down the candlelit aisle of the small wedding chapel as my radiant bride of twenty years walked toward me.

I took Sonya's hand and re-experienced the awe of that evening years earlier when we chose to make our two lives one.

I looked into her eyes and repeated my promise and commitment to love and cherish her from this day forward.

Then, I placed a ring on her finger.

For a moment, I looked at the brilliant symbol of a marriage we thought had been lost. And now was found.

7

"It Can't End Like That!"

I did not pick these men. They were delivered by fate . . . but I know them in a way I know no other men. I have never since given anyone such trust. They were willing to guard something more precious than my life. They would have carried my reputation, the memory of me. It was part of the bargain we all made, the reason we were so willing to die for one another. . . .

As long as I have memory, I will think of them all, every day. I am sure that when I leave this world, my last thoughts will be of my family—and my comrades, such good men.

—MICHAEL NORMAN, *THESE GOOD MEN*[1]

Standing with my bride at the altar in 1988 was easy. Surviving the years that led up to it (especially when my past finally caught up to me) was another story.

I had moved to Portland with visions of being the real estate emperor of the North. After I saved Oregon from economic ruin, I would expand my empire into Washington and Idaho. I had dreams of owning equity, gold chains, and big cars. I came home from the men's conference in Cannon Beach seriously aware that I was killing myself trying to keep a bunch of terminally ill properties on life-support. That's when my boss, Peter Bedford, offered to move me to the San Francisco Bay area and promote me to the position of vice president for property management.

Dreading another move, another change of school for the kids, another adjustment for Sonya, I wasn't sure I could say yes. Once I thought about the one hundred thousand dollar salary, however, I couldn't say no.

In May 1984 we made the move to a five-bedroom home three houses up from the tennis courts at the Roundhill Country Club in Alamo, California. I was living large, and I wanted my family to enjoy it. I promised to build them a swimming pool by July 4. It was only six weeks away, and we hadn't even moved in.

With a cellular phone in my hand I was dangerous. My way of putting three teams of subcontractors to work was to have them all pull up to the house at once. On Monday morning, parking and civility were nowhere to be found. The roofers, landscapers, and movers were at each other's throats. When the backhoe operator showed up to dig the pool, I could have sold ringside tickets to neighbors who didn't want to miss the fight. Eventually, peace broke out. On the Fourth, Sonya, the kids, and I splashed in our new black-bottom pool.

The Lord knows I needed to cool down.

The dreaded C word

One afternoon I came home from work around four o'clock. Everyone was gone. I clicked on the television, turned up the stereo, then grabbed the newspaper and began flipping through sections while standing at the kitchen counter.

"Why are you antsy? Why can't you just sit in one place?" I thought.

I was restless, and I didn't know why. I had a well-paid, semi-fulfilling job, a BMW 520e, a home on a spacious, green golf course where I enjoyed brisk morning walks and marvelous sunrises, and two teenage children who, occasionally, still looked forward to going on vacation with Mom and Dad.

Publicly, we seemed the model family. We were active members of a prestigious church. We enjoyed tennis at the club, growing friendships, and an expanding bank account. But when it was just the four of us, I tended to give orders, not affirmations. My empathy, patience, and ability to listen were in short supply. Family dinner conversations ended abruptly when the kids tried to squirm away from the table like roaches in a ship's galley when the light comes on.

Privately, Sonya and I were still struggling. On a one-to-ten scale of "How would you rate the quality of your marriage?" ours felt like a five that had improved to a five-and-a-half. Our communication resembled two people learning to juggle porcupines. Neither of us felt comfortable sharing emotions. We often wondered how our relationship, which could occasionally be so good, feel so bad, so much of the time. I had never paid a lot of attention to the silent, awkward passages in our marriage. To me they were like an annoying car rattle. As long as the engine wasn't on fire, I wasn't going to bother to open the hood.

Sonya would cry, and I would ask, "What's wrong?"

"Something's not working. We're not working together, Jim. I think it would help us if we saw a counselor."

Sonya had brought up the *C* word a number of times before, beginning in Lake Oswego. While I didn't argue with her, I certainly hadn't encouraged her to rush right out and make an appointment for us. The *idea* of counseling did have some appeal. I thought of a few men whose wives had asked them about going to counseling. "If you go," they told me, "it might help get her off your back."

After Cannon Beach, I couldn't use that line, because on that weekend I couldn't run any longer from the truth that God loved me, and that He wanted me to love my wife. The bottom line was I wanted Sonya to be happier. *I* wanted to be happier, and I wanted our marriage to be better.

We began to see a counselor named Bonnie Daniel. She put us at ease and invited us to begin talking. Along the way, Sonya and I began to listen to each other, and the light bulbs began to come on:

How both Sonya and I came with personal liabilities that we had brought into the marriage.

How I could be so convincing to my wife that she didn't see my "reasoning" for what it was: manipulation.

Why Sonya had difficulty identifying and expressing her needs to me as they arose but instead stuffed them inside until they eventually erupted in tears and led to depression.

The sessions with Bonnie left us enlightened—and exhausted. They exposed our "hot" buttons, our tendencies, and our needs. Counseling stripped us of our masks, providing us a progressively larger peek into our true selves and the reality that we were imperfect yet worthy of each other's love. I knew something was getting through to me, because some nights on my way home from work, I would pull into the grocery store just to buy a bouquet of flowers. Spontaneous hugs in the kitchen were taken off the endangered species list. When Sonya or I would fall back into our old communication patterns, we would try to find a way to talk—and work—them out.

But there was a lot more to be done.

Skies partly overcast

Almost immediately during those first sessions, Bonnie detected something in my twisted body language and clipped words. She suggested that I come back, alone. With Sonya's encouragement, and quiet apprehension, I did.

Bonnie plunged right in. "Jim, you haven't talked much about your dad. How would you evaluate your relationship with him?"

I had been thinking about it for months.

And for the next few weeks, Bonnie steered me onto a path of rediscovered emotions and new understanding. We talked about my painful lack of relationship with Dad, his alcoholism, and how it made me feel growing up. I shared the fearful unpredictability of his personality that oscillated between humor and hostility, and how it was usually determined by how many stops he made on his way home from work. We talked about some of the protective behaviors that I had taken on to cope with the craziness that seemed to be going on at home but which no one wanted to talk about.

Telling the stories was like rethreading the projector and sitting through bad home movies. Each reel, each session, made a little more sense. I replayed early memories with family members—grandparents, uncles, my brother, Scott, and my sister, Nancy—until I began to see the flickering images of my life. And with Bonnie's help, a scratchy moving picture emerged.

My dad didn't invent his anger, he simply inherited it. And in our family it was a "gift" that kept on giving. My grandfather had received it from his mother, whose harsh expectations dominated the Horsley family's early history in southeastern Idaho. Dad escaped by joining the Navy and, following his time at Officer Candidate School, got married and spent World War II in San Francisco. His drinking started during the war and never stopped when he returned home.

I'd usually leave Bonnie's office as calm as I had walked in. The following morning I would rise before the sun and walk around the golf course. That's when I began to process some of my emotions about Dad and the events and circumstances I experienced while growing up. Thirty years of bottled up emotion had fermented into anger that masked a much deeper hurt, and loss of not having had the kind of accepting, affirming relationship any son wants with his father.

I felt anger at my grandfather for how he'd treated my dad. Angry at Dad for the tyrant he had been with me. Angry at Mom for not confronting our family's reality, and angry at myself for. . . .

At that moment I stopped, and thought of Jeff and Shannon. I remembered a recent afternoon when I had wanted them to do what I asked.

"I told you to get going. Now move!" They resentfully started to get on with it when I overheard Sonya, who had been inside the house, ask Shannon, "What's going on?"

"I guess we didn't salute Dad fast enough."

I was the tyrant. I was passing on something destructive to *my* children. I noticed its effect more clearly on Shannon than Jeff. He would opt for a passive and sullen response. By Shannon's early teens, it was clear to me she had already begun to inherit my gift of deflection and a biting tongue. She could be feisty and fiery, and often we sparred with testy looks and defiant words.

One day she told me she was going to a party where her friends were serving beer. "But," she stressed, "I'm not going to drink any." I was baffled.

"That's just like setting your plane on fire before you launch yourself off the carrier," I said. "Why would you want to do it?" I never considered that Shannon might be going to the party because she wanted to build relationships with kids. I only wanted to prove my point.

One day, after the two of us failed to hear each other out, Shannon looked at me and calmly asked, "Dad, what color is the sky in the world you live in?" It wasn't a flip remark. It was a daughter asking, "Dad, for a moment, could you just try and have enough empathy to know what my life is like and what I have to deal with?"

Her remark really shook me up. I didn't want to lose a daughter. I wanted to love her, and I deeply wanted her to love me. I struggled to know where to start. I felt so much underlying tension in my life that it was hard to see which issue I needed to tackle first, much less explore what color the sky was in my world.

I was forty-two years old. I had handled combat, flown with the Blues, and was now getting paid six figures to roll the dice in a real-life Monopoly game. And for the first time I was able to look at the communication breakdowns and struggles in my marriage. For the first time I had begun to feel a father's wrath and then discovered I was passing it on to my own children. For the first time I was finding the freedom to feel what was really going on inside me. Little did I know where it was all leading.

"This was your dad...."

On the morning of Memorial Day 1989, I walked out on to the patio in my cut-offs, T-shirt, and thongs. My only agenda was to drink a glass of chilled orange juice with Sonya and read the morning newspaper. I had seen something about a ceremony that day in nearby Concord.

"It will only take a few minutes to get there," I said to Sonya. "Why don't we go?"

The cemetery that morning was still. A small collection of people sat in rows of folding chairs facing a manicured green hillside dotted with headstones and small American flags. Sonya and I got out of the car and walked to the edge of the crowd. The ceremony seemed to be winding down. At the microphone, a silver-haired veteran talked about his memories of several friends who had died in the Pacific. He spoke in reverent tones as if they were still alive. To him, they were.

After he sat down, a younger man in an Army fatigue jacket and dungarees took the mike. A red bandana stretched across his forehead, and his right arm sported a collection of tattoos.

"I was in 'Nam," he said. "I couldn't resist coming up here. But I gotta tell you, events like this bug me. They're like the freekin' jungle where I got shot. They're bad berries. They're tea parties for soldiers that are long gone. The only guys that have any sense left in them are sitting over there at the picnic tables. You go ahead and wave your flags. I'll toast one to you with some cold sixteen ouncers."

The vet hadn't walked beyond the first row of stunned listeners when I turned to Sonya and said, "I can't let it end like this."

I stood up and walked forward, my thongs slapping the cement. I had no idea what I was going to say until I picked up the microphone, which felt heavy in my cold, nervous hands.

"I can appreciate some of the rancor this young man expressed," I said, clearing my dry throat. "But you need to understand it wasn't just those in the ground forces who died in Vietnam. I served in the Navy as a pilot on a carrier, and we lost over twenty guys. Today, I think of them.

"That's all I really want to say. Just thanks for putting on this event. Not only did a lot of vets get hurt, but a lot of families and friends suffered with them. Today is a day for all of us."

Someone read a prayer, and the ceremony ended. A few minutes later, as people began to go back to their cars, a woman walked up to me. Tears were running down her cheeks. She didn't introduce herself but simply reached out, hugged me, and continued to cry. Then, she stepped back and wiped her eyes.

"My husband was one of the Navy pilots killed in a terrible fire on the USS *Enterprise*. I was pregnant at the time, and our son is now at the Naval Academy."

I remembered the accounts of the tragedy, and nodded.

Unbelievably, she was telling another story. In this woman I saw the face of Tonya Clark, who had been pregnant when Arlo and I sailed off to North Vietnam on the *Midway*. Six months before Arlo died flying over enemy skies, Tonya had given birth to a baby boy, Tad. He was now sixteen years old.

It all hit me at once—the feelings, the similarity between her husband and son, and Arlo and Tad.

"Would it have been important," I asked this woman, "for your son to have known something about his father?"

"Absolutely," she said. "It would be one of the best things that could ever happen in his life."

That was all I needed to hear. As Sonya and I drove back home, I couldn't stop thinking about Tonya and Tad. In all the years since Vietnam, it had never occurred to me, until now, that Tad had grown up without knowing his father.

Following the end of the war, Tonya had moved from Whidbey Island and had endured some rough relationships along the way. We had kept in sporadic contact through Christmas cards, but I hadn't talked to her in years.

There was only one thing to do. Once home, I managed to track down her Seattle phone number and telephoned her.

"Tonya, this is Jim." We briefly caught up on the past ten years, and then I got to the reason for my call.

"Tonya, I have no idea what it's been like for you raising a son by yourself, but I'm sure it's not been easy. I need to ask you a question. Do you think Tad would appreciate hearing something about his dad?"

She hesitated for a few seconds. "I think he really would," she said. "In fact, I know he would."

"I have an idea. . . ." I invited her and Tad to spend a weekend with our family in the east bay. "I could show you the city. We could sit out on the patio and share some stories. We've got plenty of room and want you to feel like family," I said.

"I'll ask Tad and call you back."

Several weeks later, on a Sunday afternoon, I met Tonya and Tad at the airport and drove them to our home. The next day I took off work, and we visited Ghiardelli Square, where Arlo, Tonya, Sonya, and I, along with eighteen-month-old Jeff, had lingered that afternoon back in 1972. I took them to Sausalito and then drove by Jackie Jensen's Restaurant in Oakland's Jack London Square. It was a chance to get reacquainted with Tonya and an opportunity for Tad to see the places his dad and I had known.

The next day, we sat at the shaded patio table in our backyard. It was early afternoon, and the sun reflected brightly off the shimmering pool. At my side was a black plastic briefcase, which had been kind of a miniature Smithsonian Museum of maps, newspaper clippings, and dog-eared snapshots of my time in Vietnam. I didn't know for sure what was inside. I had never really sorted it all out. If Tad was to know something about the mustachioed twenty-five-year-old pilot in the picture, I would need to provide the captions.

I looked at Tonya, then Tad. "Would you be interested in hearing about what probably happened to your dad on his last flight?"

"I would," said Tonya. "All I remember is that it was January 10, 1973. It was at night and the plane was near a place called Vinh. That's really all I know."

"Then this is the first time you've ever heard the story in any detail?" I asked.

Tonya nodded. I lifted the dusty briefcase onto the table, clicked open the two latches, and lifted the lid on a small, round hill of papers. Tad leaned forward.

I unfolded a tattered map of North Vietnam, annotated with symbols for surface-to-air missile sights our squadron had set out to destroy, or avoid. I pointed to places where the *Midway* had been positioned, and where Arlo first flew into the war.

"This is the hourglass section of the North Vietnam coast

where your dad had mapped out radar checkpoints for night strike ingress routes.

"This is the Route Pack VI region, where he flew a majority of his missions in the A-6 Intruder.

"This is the route into Hanoi where your dad dodged enemy fire and SAMS on a multi-plane daylight strike we both participated in."

Then I pointed at a spot on the map so automatically, I didn't have to find the name.

"This is the area near Vinh. Your dad and Mike McCormick were scheduled to attack a military training and weapons storage facility just on the back side of this ridge line." I pointed to a section of the map just fifty miles inland from Brandon Bay, the site where I thought we had lost Slick when his wing went up in flames ten months earlier.

"The *Midway* was operating on a midnight to noon schedule. Bob Ponton and I had flown a strike on the first launch cycle against another target in the same general vicinity your dad was scheduled to attack on the second cycle. Earlier that evening, after finishing our planning for the upcoming flights, your dad and I had grabbed a hamburger and played a game of Acey Deucey before heading for our bunkroom to get some sleep. We had talked about the difficulty of trying to get to our targets because of the low cloud deck and poor visibility.

"When I returned from my flight about one-thirty that morning, I hit the sack for a couple of hours until my next scheduled flight at eight o'clock. I had only been asleep two hours when the squadron duty officer woke me up and told me that your dad's plane hadn't made it back to the carrier."

Tad showed little emotion. Yet, he seemed deeply engaged in every fact, as if trying to picture the fatal flight for the first time. I could see his eyes darting back and forth, from the map, to me, then to his mother. Her eyes were moist. So were mine. I began to describe the scene in the ready room in those pre-dawn hours when we had learned of Arlo's downed plane.

"I hastily briefed for a search-and-rescue mission and raced up to the flight deck for a pre-dawn launch."

I got only as far as the second sentence, when the tears began to stream down my cheeks.

I was back in the cockpit of the A-6, streaking north of Vinh, looking for any sign of two fellow pilots, two friends, who were never coming home again. The only time I had let myself feel Arlo's death was on that search-and-rescue flight. Orbiting the target area in the clouds, oblivious to the anti-aircraft fire, I wept into my oxygen mask as we unsuccessfully attempted to establish radio contact with them. Then, I could hide my emotions behind the protective visor that covered my face.

Now some seventeen years later, the visor was up. I had told the story to others, but I had never allowed the story to speak to me. To my surprise, the grief had not gone away. It was as real as the look on Tad's face that said, "Tell me more."

I obliged. I pulled out a handful of snapshots. One by one, I set them on the table for Tad to see. "The *Midway* had departed the combat zone for Singapore four days before Christmas, 1972. I don't know if you can tell by these pictures, but we weren't exactly Boy Scouts." I had firsthand proof to go with each photo.

One was a shot of Arlo with a drink in his hand on the tenth floor of the Shangri-la Hotel in Singapore. On that New Year's Eve, we dropped so many empty glasses from our window on the sidewalks below that it sounded like exploding firecrackers.

When the sun came up, we headed for the hotel's pitch-and-putt golf course to play for breakfast. The rest of the day was spent in bed before heading back to the ship and the war.

Tad picked up each photo and looked at it closely. When I told him his dad specialized in impish irreverence, this sixteen-year-old boy with a bright shock of red hair and thin, sharp features leaned back and laughed. When he smiled, I could see Arlo's face all over again. Though some of my recollections sometimes embellished a bit of the truth, I wanted Tad to be sure of one thing.

"Your dad was not a hero," I said. "I'm not a hero. But you need to understand that your dad was my closest friend. He was a guy like me, with traits and rough edges. Hopefully, he is a little less of a question mark to you now."

I reached across the table and put a few of the photos in Tad's hands.

"These are for you."

He looked down and smiled. "Thank you very much. Thanks for doing this."

All I had done was arrange a little family reunion—and embrace a piece of who I really was in front of people I really cared about.

The darkest hour

After Tonya and Tad flew home, I stuffed Vietnam back in my briefcase. Though the lid clicked shut, something had now been opened. That fall, Sonya and I drove Jeff to San Luis Obispo, where he was starting his first year of college. I had finished an early morning jog, and Sonya and I were in our motel room, getting ready for parent orientation. Sonya's hair dryer dueled with the television for my attention. I glanced at the screen and a news graphic: "Lexington, Kentucky—Vietnam Remembered." I moved to the edge of the bed and turned up the volume.

The scene was a downtown memorial park. A man about my age read from a list of names, slowly and deliberately:

William. . . .
Steven. . . .
Douglas. . . .

In the background a bugle man played *Taps*.

Michael. . . .
Jonathan. . . .

Without knowing who the people were, recognizing only that they were young men and women who lost their lives in Vietnam, I broke down. I put my head in my hands, and I sobbed. The news story ended, but I continued to cry. It felt heavy and dark, like a river of immense sadness and grief. Unsure where it was coming from, I traced back to the tributaries:

A year earlier I had visited a replica of the Vietnam Memorial Wall in Sacramento. When I ran my fingers over the names of former squadron mates, Lt. Raymond P. Donnelly, LTJG Michael S. Bixel, LTJG Robert A. Clark, Lt. Michael T. McCormick, and others from our airwing who hadn't come home, the memory of the war triggered something deep inside me. That was the first trickle.

During the visit with Tonya and Tad more feelings had begun to flow.

Now, in the motel room, a wider sorrow spilled out.

I wasn't sure what to do with it, so I dressed it up every morning in a three-piece suit. At work I was the good soldier, tracking income, impressing tenants, maintaining a full and varied menu of executive power lunches. I did everything needed to ensure the proper care and feeding of six million square feet of commercial property.

The home front enjoyed relative calm. The climate of communication with Sonya stayed moderately warm. Every so often I would make history by asking Sonya out on a date. Shannon would applaud from the front porch as I called out from the car, "I promise to have her home by eleven."

Inside me, a war was going on. Though no one in my immediate circle had experienced the war, there was one person I could talk to. His name was Max Carey. He had been stationed on the *Midway* with me as an A-7 pilot flying with VA-56 during our combat tour in Vietnam and the ship's deployment to Japan following the war. Max had been an all-Ivy league defensive back on Columbia's football team. He was exceptionally bright, and his effervescent personality made him the hit of every party. I had flown to Atlanta for a job interview toward the end of my tour with the Blues, and Max and I had gone out for dinner and rehashed our old war stories.

In mid-1989, I noticed his picture on the cover of *INC.* magazine that included an article he had written called "The Superman Complex." Max Carey was a golden boy. He came back from Vietnam a hero. He single-handedly saved his business from going under. But the trauma of both experiences eventually caught up with Carey and forced him to take an unsparing look at who he was and admit that he was not a Superman, and that he could not go it alone anymore.

Max had put his life savings and a 150,000-dollar loan into a start-up company and then saw it all crumble. The bottom dropped out in January 1982, four months after our exuberant night on the town together. In the article, he made the point that "if it hadn't been for the added stress of trying to save his company, the grief and fear he'd buried from his Vietnam War days might never have surfaced." He talked about coming to terms through counseling with his "delayed-stress syndrome," and how the discovery of his need to become real was the key to putting his life and business back in order. He had put enormous energy into bringing public attention to the needs of other veterans, and finding unique ways to help them find the healing he had experienced.

I phoned him to talk about the article, and we had a very enlightening conversation about his emotional struggle with his combat experience. His comments were very supportive in convincing me that what I was beginning to feel was real.

On a Tuesday a couple of weeks later, I was listening to a local talk-show radio program while driving to a business meeting. An author, Mike Norman, was being interviewed about his newly released book *These Good Men.* Norman was a former Marine sergeant who had fought in Vietnam. His story was about men whose lives had hemorrhaged in a North Vietnamese Army ambush in 1968, at Bridge 28. He had spent several years tracking down and documenting the current lives of those who had survived, and found many of them to still be bleeding.

Later that day, I purchased a copy and began reading. It wasn't a war story. It was a story about men that fit exactly what Jimmy Doolittle was talking about when he made the statement, "There are two emotions that bring people together. One is love, and the other is shared adversity."

I couldn't put the book down. By Friday evening, one passage in the last chapter silenced me to the core. As Norman wrote about the reunion of Vietnam veterans, he described a particular moment of the gathering as one of the men honors his friends by saying, "I think we should offer a toast . . . to our comrades . . . we left behind."

I felt like the wind had been knocked out of me. I could feel a surge of emotion deep in my gut. I couldn't concentrate on the final pages. Instead, I said goodnight to Sonya, dragged myself off the couch, and headed to bed.

The next morning I woke up in a state of mental exhaustion. I was alone in the house. Sonya was at work, Shannon was with friends, and Jeff was away at college. Unable to concentrate even on the sports section of the newspaper, I put on my gym shorts and running shoes, and opened the front door. It was a perfect day for a jog. I stretched for a couple of minutes and crossed the street for the park, hoping that a couple of miles of exercise would jolt me out of my lethargy.

Breaking into a slow trot, I didn't get farther than the end of the next block.

All of a sudden I was unable to run another step. A heaviness fell over my body. It was like someone had draped a thick coat of chains over me.

I bent over and tried to take a deep breath. A couple of runners zipped past me on the park trail and gave me a quizzical look. I couldn't have cared less what I looked like. My only concern was how I was going to get back home.

I felt dead. I could barely pick up my feet. Normally, the sight of me shuffling slowly across the street to the house would have been an amusing scene, except that I felt so depleted and lifeless. Thankfully, I finally reached the front door.

Entering the living room, I sprawled out on the soft carpet thinking that might help me relax. The emotional pain felt like it was crushing me. Even our dog's concerned licking didn't stir me. After ten minutes or so, I stripped down for a shower. I leaned against the wall, hoping the hot water would somehow rejuvenate me.

I got dressed and went into the kitchen to make some coffee, but I wasn't feeling a bit better. Slumping down on the kitchen chair, the only thing I could think of was Bonnie Daniel's suggestion, "If you're ever having a problem, call this number." I hesitatingly picked up the phone and dialed her pager. When her recorded voice greeted me I punched in my number, fully expecting she would call back the next day.

Ten minutes later the phone rang.

"Hello, this is the Horsley residence."

"Jim, this is Bonnie. What's happening?"

I paused, unable to speak.

I started to sob and couldn't stop. I heard the painful, fragile cries of a broken, helpless man who had nowhere to turn. The dam was finally breaking. The release had finally come.

Hunched over, eyes closed, I wondered if I was going to make it.

"Jim, I want you to lock on to something that's real right now. The countertop. The kitchen sink." Anything.

I stared at the clock on the built-in oven.

For the next ten minutes, Bonnie kept me on life support.

"You've got to take care of yourself, Jim. Just take it very easy. Don't do anything strenuous."

I didn't fight. I had done enough of that in another world.

I wanted to eject from the darkness. I couldn't articulate what was happening, but I had a wife and children who said they loved me. And I had never needed that assurance more than now.

The abyss of that morning widened at night for the next couple of weeks. Early in the morning I would wake up sobbing, and Sonya would hold me. Those were the blackest hours, when I curled up in my memory and found the words of another's sorrow echoing my own.

> I am worn out from groaning; all night long I flood my bed with weeping and drench my couch with tears. My eyes grow weak with sorrow; they fail because of all my foes. (Psalm 6:6–7)

> The cords of death entangled me; the torrents of destruction overwhelmed me. The cords of the grave coiled around me; the snares of death confronted me. In my distress I called to the LORD; I cried to my God for help. From his temple he heard my voice; my cry came before him, into his ears. (Psalm 18:4–6)

In my grief, I found the company of hope. Hope I couldn't let go of, because I knew two things were still true: my wife's loving, warm embrace, and God's tender presence, which had never seemed more real. And there was something else.

On a sunny afternoon, I had been able to tell Tonya the legacy of her husband and introduce a father to a son. I had found a way to step outside my comfort zone and lift up my visor. I had found a different kind of courage.

8

The Ultimate Gift

Charity. To love human beings in so far as they are nothing. That is to love them as God does.

—SIMONE WEIL[1]

The Vietnam War had created a bit of a problem, because now I was living two separate existences. On the outside, I was still functioning and going to work every day. People called me for advice. I cracked jokes and churned out memos. I was still way too demanding on others and myself.

Inside I was a walking wreck. Once I chose to be honest, once I chose to lift the visor on who I really was and how I really felt, I couldn't turn around. I couldn't pour my grief back in the bottle, because it was still spilling out. I didn't know how much longer it would continue, but I knew I wanted it to end.

But more than that, I wanted to know what it all really meant. I wanted to wake up one morning and have its impact on my life make sense. I could endure my residual restlessness—for awhile. I just wanted to arrive at a place of relative calm—inside myself, and with my world.

139

I had a few loose ends I needed to close. A couple I knew about, the other I didn't.

Granite reflections

Though I had never met the soldiers in Mike Norman's book, I wanted what they had. I wanted to discover what Max Carey had talked about in his *INC.* magazine article. I wanted the opportunity to be open, to be vulnerable, to be myself.

The Monday following Bonnie Daniel's life-saving effort, I called Max.

"There's a book I've just finished reading that you might appreciate," I told him. It's called *These Good Men*.

Max laughed. "You're not going to believe this," he said, "but I went to college with the author. As a matter of fact, in two weeks, Mike is going to convene another reunion with the guys he wrote about. It's going to be here in Atlanta. I'd like you to come too."

I told him I couldn't. I was up to my eyeballs at work, and I didn't want to intrude on the intimacy of someone else's group. And besides, I didn't have the money.

"Think about coming down," said Max. "The residue of Vietnam you're dealing with inside is real. Pay attention to it."

A few days later, an airplane ticket, courtesy of Max's frequent flyer miles, arrived in my mailbox.

At the reunion of Mike Norman and his comrades, I met complete strangers with whom I could identify immediately. We had nothing in common, and yet we had everything in common. Some of the guys were pretty rough around the edges, as if they were still feeling the hangover from Vietnam. Some had never put down their beers. They gathered around Formica tables and raw memories. Their recollections flowed. So did their tears. One man's story would get derailed by another man's remark, until both were walking together, again, in the same Vietnamese village.

Sometimes I leaned forward. Eventually I had to get up from my chair and go back to my hotel room, where I was content to be alone. I entered into my own silent reunion with McCormick, Clark, Bixel, and Donnelly. I saw their stubble, and smelled their aftershave, and I wished like hell that they would have survived.

To keep me company, I opened up my worn pocket Bible and turned again to so many of the words I had underlined in pencil. Psalm 31 captured my emotions:

> Be merciful to me, O LORD, for I am in distress; my eyes grow weak with sorrow, my soul and my body with grief. (v.9)

I was reading about myself.

> I will be glad and rejoice in your love, for you saw my affliction and knew the anguish of my soul. You have not handed me over to the enemy but have set my feet in a spacious place. (vs. 7–8)

I was coming home. Home to the grieving I had stored but never unpacked. Home to the pain I had felt and not been able to comprehend. It was a trek home on the longest journey of all. Back to a bitter source of sorrow I had never wanted to look in the eye.

As I found the courage to feel the losses in my life, the grief that had been surging inside for so long began to subside. I could feel some of it leave that weekend in Atlanta. Over the next several weeks, I began to make peace with a past I couldn't change. I attended the National Prayer Breakfast in Washington, D.C. Instead of flying home on Thursday following the breakfast, I stayed through the weekend for a serendipitous Friday evening reunion with Jerry and Delores Franz, my former Billings Young

Life leaders, who had worked behind the scenes organizing the breakfast.

Just after dawn the next morning, I drove from the hotel toward the Lincoln Memorial and parked next to the curb. It was a cold, steel-gray day, and the wind was howling. I left the car and began walking toward the clearing sprinkled with tall bare trees that twisted in the wind.

I couldn't see it, but I knew I was close, because in the distance I could see the three bronzed figures in the tree line pointing the way, standing as sentinels over the Vietnam Memorial below them. Then, I saw the two polished black granite walls etched with the names of fifty-eight thousand men and women. In the granite reflections I could see the flag and three soldiers. I walked down the long, sloping, cement path to the Monument's most recessed place, where the names of America's last casualties rested. I knew where to look. I got on my knees and touched the names of the last two A-6 Intruder pilots to die in the war.

Robert A. Clark.

Michael T. McCormick.

Alone in the silence, I knelt and wept. This time, however, I didn't feel weary of heart. I felt whole. For years I had denied the loss of my friends, and the pain of their deaths. After seventeen years of suppression and denial, I could finally say good-bye. And begin the healing.

Going public

As the winter of 1990 yielded to spring, I could feel the years of hardness and anger I had buried beginning to melt. In my early morning conversations and journaling with God, I began to grasp some understanding of the journey I'd taken. It was a trip uncompleted, but I'd come a long way.

My public speaking activity had continued to increase, and my stories of flying and faith were usually well received. But I felt a need to be more transparent about some of the difficult things I had been experiencing. I sensed it was more important to speak out of my incompleteness than to try always to appeal to others through my strengths.

In early April, I received a speaking invitation from Scott Farmer, an associate pastor at Menlo Park Presbyterian Church. He wanted me to give a presentation to a large group at his monthly breakfast gathering at a Palo Alto area Holiday Inn. I had shared with Scott earlier some of the personal struggles I had been dealing with over the previous year. During our conversation about the breakfast, he said, "Jim, I've heard you speak and have enjoyed hearing about your personal testimony, but I want you to consider talking to our group about the 'so what?' aspects of your faith. What difference has your Christian faith made in how you've dealt with some of the recent emotions related to Vietnam?"

The chance to speak was an opportunity to be vulnerable with others, not at the expense of someone else, or to attribute some of the pain I'd experienced to circumstances, but to speak honestly and simply out of what I had experienced and what it could mean for others. In this sense, I wanted to echo Henri Nouwen's words: "Making one's own wounds a source of healing does not call for a sharing of superficial, personal pains, but for a constant willingness to see one's pain and suffering as rising from the depth of the human condition which all men share."[2]

Six weeks later on a Friday morning, I walked to the podium in a large banquet room filled with 275 business and professional men and women. I told them about a journey I wanted them to take with me, to discover what my life as a former Blue Angel had been like above the clouds and behind the stick, but more importantly, what my life consisted of "inside the man."

I provided some insider stories and perspectives about my two years with the Blue Angels. I explained how we had pursued the ultimate in perfection while performing outside our comfort zone. And I said, "As exciting as the experience was, I paid a price by damaging relationships that were ultimately much more important. It wasn't until I found the courage to confront the reality of who I had become that I was able to find reconciliation with God and a family who loved me."

Then I walked forward on the platform and looked intently at the faces in front of me. I shared the struggle and pain of reconciling the experiences of my past. I talked about the pain of a broken relationship with my father, and the loss of my most trusted friends in combat, how I had gone to Vietnam believing that good guys win and life is fair, and found out that neither was true.

"The young men and women we sent to Vietnam may not have been America's best," I said, "but on the day they died, they were as good as they would ever be, for each other. And when I came home, I brought part of them with me, and left part of me behind."

Then I shared about coming to terms with my grief related to a loss of innocence and the loss of four buddies in combat. I talked about "the wars of abuse, abandonment, illness, and broken relationships that each of us face."

I ended by talking about hope.

"Today, because of Christ's sufficiency in my time of complete insufficiency, my frightening emotional brokenness resulted in a degree of spiritual intimacy with God and relational intimacy with Sonya that I had never experienced. I discovered an empathy and compassion that is enabling me to relate, for the first time, to the pain and needs of others. And it is beginning to make an extraordinary difference in my life.

"The opportunity to find God sufficient for our deepest needs is available to everyone in this room. But it requires a willingness to step outside our comfort zone, and deal with some of the painful realities that we ignore in our pursuit of fame, fortune, power, or pleasure we've made so important.

"God offers the hope of love, and the hope of eternity that is available to each of us. But it's your choice. I'm here to encourage you to make it."

For the first time in my four years of public speaking, I saw the story of God's faithfulness in the midst of my vulnerability register in the eyes and emotions of my audience. A few days later, I presented a similar message at a men's breakfast in the nearby city of Fremont. Toward the end of my talk, I noticed a heavyset bearded man walk quickly out of the room. After my speech I stayed to talk with a few men who wanted to know more about the odds of survival for pilots who chose to eject.

A few days later I received a letter from a man who had been in the audience. The letter was full of pain. The man closed by asking, "How do you let go of it?" That day I contacted him, and we agreed to meet. When he came to my office, I could see he was the man at the breakfast who had left the room. He introduced himself as Russ Donnicci, and I liked him immediately. Regardless of what was going on in his life, he had a warm twinkle in his eye and a wonderful smile. And he had no trouble telling me his story. . . .

Russ had lived in Fremont most of his life. His best friend, a kid named Ernie, went to fight in Vietnam after high school graduation. Within weeks of Ernie's seeing combat action, the word reached Russ: Ernie had been killed in action.

Russ was already scheduled to enter the Army. "As soon as I could, I volunteered to go to Vietnam. I figured it would be easy to get even," said Russ. "After several months in Saigon, I came back to the states on leave to get married, and then went AWOL. I just wanted a few more days before going back. The

Army couldn't believe my attitude, and they couldn't wait to get rid of me. I was treated as expendable and left Vietnam as a private."

"Jim, I have never been able to deal with the loss of Ernie, or the survivor's guilt I feel. Whenever I hear Ernie's name I break down in tears. It doesn't matter where I am, at work or at home. A sound or a smell can trigger a memory, good or bad. I thought I had put most of it behind me, but it is still swallowing me. It's like a knife; it just keeps twisting and twisting.

"The only way I can handle it is to keep myself busy with activities and work. I know my pain is growing and my anger is affecting my life and my family. My wife has been encouraging me for several years to get some help, but I have been resisting. I just haven't thought anyone would understand."

Russ began coming by my office weekly to talk, and over the course of the next few weeks, several other veterans who we'd come in contact with joined us as well.

For most of them, regardless of what they had been doing that week, even the simplest errands, conversation somehow came back to Vietnam. We discussed our backgrounds. We talked about wartime buddies and painful memories. We shared our anger, our fears, and our relational nightmares. But we also laughed and experienced the warmth of the bonding that had occurred so quickly. Sometimes they wept, and I wept with them. I facilitated our gatherings, and would spend a small portion of each session talking about God's forgiveness, mercy, and acceptance. A few of the men circled around spiritual matters from a distance. They seemed like wary gulls who looked down at busy fishermen, and yet saw nothing for dinner.

One day Russ seemed on the verge of a semi-major meltdown. He had become increasingly introspective. And although fairly well grounded in his Christian faith, he was struggling with questions that seemed unanswered, especially in the area of forgiveness. I listened, and then recalled some words the apostle Paul had said that related to his own pain and torment.

"Paul wanted some relief, and three times he pleaded with the Lord to take it away from him," I said to Russ, "but God responded, not by giving him what he asked for, but by saying, 'My grace is sufficient for you, for my power is made perfect in weakness' [2 Corinthians 12:9]."

Russ didn't buy it, and fired back, "His grace doesn't feel sufficient right now. I can't let go, and I want this pain out of my life."

"What have you been doing about it?" I asked.

"I've been praying," he replied.

I felt an impulse.

"Why don't you ask God again, right now?"

"What do you mean?" Russ asked.

"Let's assume that Jesus is sitting right here in the empty chair next to you. What would you want to ask Him?"

Russ gave me kind of a strange look, and took a deep breath. "Lord, I'm tired of this pain. I've lived with it for too long."

Even though Russ was still facing me, I could tell his words were landing in the empty chair.

"I know what I'm doing is unhealthy," he continued. "My family can see it. I can see it. I know You're real. I've entrusted my life to You. Lord, I'm laying this at the foot of Your cross. It's Yours, and I need Your help."

He ended, and we all sat there in the silence. When I looked up, Russ was wiping his eyes. He seemed tired and yet tremendously relieved. I felt another impulse.

"Have you ever said good-bye to Ernie?" Russ looked at me, absorbing the question slowly. "Have you ever talked about, or written about, what his death means?"

Russ remained puzzled. "No, I never have."

"What if you wrote him a good-bye letter," I said. "You wouldn't have to keep packing around all of those feelings you have for him. You could let them fall onto the page. It might be cathartic for you, and it would help give you closure."

I could see that Russ was nodding yes with his eyes. He said he'd think about it.

The next time we got together he sat down and said, "I wrote the letter, and then I read it out loud. It felt hard, sad, and good all at once, but I'm glad I did it."

"Have you ever thought of visiting Ernie's grave?" If he had, Russ didn't let on. He said that if he decided to go, he didn't want to go alone and would want to take his wife, Debi, with him. The cemetery was just up the road. On a Sunday afternoon, Russ found Ernie's marker. He and Debi laid a small bouquet of flowers at the grave. They stayed long enough for Russ to remember the good times they shared and to say good-bye.

The following week, Russ talked some more, and we traded stories of vets we had lost touch with. We talked about families from our youth and about the parents of friends we had come to know.

"Have you ever seen Ernie's folks or told them how you felt about him?"

"Never have," he said. "But I've thought about them a lot. They live just fifty miles down the road in Modesto. I spoke to them not long ago. They contacted me to thank me for the Vietnam Memorial plaque I donated to our high school in Ernie's name. It lists the names of the eleven men from the school who gave their lives in the war. I couldn't bring myself to say anything more than we all miss Ernie a great deal. I was surprised they had heard about the plaque, but when it was presented to the school, Ernie's niece was a student there."

It was clear that this memory marked the beginning of his healing.

In the weeks to come, Russ's voice became softer. He could make it through a story about Ernie without crying. I felt like a confidant and coach who had helped a friend find his way through one of life's narrow, twisted ravines. I merely offered suggestions, and Russ did the walking. He wasn't afraid to stumble, or admit that he, like I, was still learning how to be the men our wives thought they had married.

"How come it's so hard for us to say how nice our wives look when they look so stunning for a night on the town?" asked Russ.

"I don't have the faintest idea," I said.

"Let's make a pledge that you and I will tell them how we really feel, and not keep it to ourselves," said Russ. I said I would join him. On his journey out of desperation, Russ Donnicci was preparing me to take the next step on my own journey to a place I thought I'd never see, again.

Until the invitation came.

A greater vision

Six months earlier, on the day after Thanksgiving in 1989, Sonya and I had closed escrow on the sale of our home. We had put it on the market because it was blatantly obvious to me that the real estate economy had entered a nosedive, and it was going to be ugly when it hit bottom.

Our thirteenth move in twenty-one years of marriage proved to be the most difficult, not because of the packing, but because for the past five years, we had finally begun to feel like we had a home. We had renewed our vows. Jeff and Shannon were able to spend their high school years in the same home, and Sonya was getting a sense of roots. But when we couldn't justify the overhead that I would need to generate to keep the black-bottom pool filled and the mortgage current, we began to look for a moving van.

The worst moment came when Sonya began filling the nail

holes in the wall where our family photos had been displayed. As she shuddered with tears, I led her to the car and sent her ahead to our next residence, five miles down the road in Danville. It wasn't any easier for me. I knew we had made the right decision, but that didn't help dislodge the baseball-sized knot in my throat.

From a six-figure lifestyle, we downsized to a three-bedroom home Sonya called "the house from hell." She was convinced the place didn't have one right angle. The foundation tilted so steeply from earlier soil settlement problems that when we set the bottom edge of our bedroom dresser against the baseboard, there were still two inches between the wall and the dresser's top edge. The house was so bent that we would get vertigo walking around the corner from the hallway to the kitchen. I thought the house just needed a little tender loving care. Sonya, on the other hand, thought it needed a bulldozer.

Then, providence caught up with me. I joined a small group of folks to attend a luncheon in Oakland for evangelist Leighton Ford. I had great respect for his integrity and warmth from our prior visits and looked forward to more time with him. At the end of our meeting, as we were headed down the hallway for the exit, he asked me, "Jim, how are you doing?" I confessed I couldn't seem to turn around without running into something related to Vietnam. Leighton gently grabbed my arm, pulled me into the men's room, and said, "Let's pray."

He prayed for healing, "for those who had been affected by the war, their families and their loved ones." And he prayed that I would be strengthened in following God's leading in whatever He had in store for me in the coming days.

Leighton's prayer deeply touched me, and as we walked down the hall, he said, "Why don't you write Bob Seiple a letter?"

"Who is he?" I asked.

"Bob is president of World Vision, one of the world's largest Christian relief and development agencies. He's a former marine aviator, and a Vietnam veteran. Why don't you write him and at least let him know what you're thinking."

On Monday, three days after I mailed my letter, his secretary called and asked me to contact Chet Starr, World Vision's fundraising representative in the Bay Area. A day later, when we talked by phone, Chet invited me to join him at a church potluck that was being held at my home church that coming Saturday night. In the most tactful way I could, I tried to tell Chet that church potlucks weren't exactly at the top of my list of weekend activities.

"You'll miss a good speaker," he said.

"Who?" I asked.

"Bob Seiple."

Suddenly, lasagna and Waldorf salad served on a paper plate sounded irresistible. I didn't know a whole lot about Bob Seiple, other than the fact that the organization he led was caring for nearly a million children a year in over ninety countries. It had all started with a little Chinese girl named White Jade.

Back in 1950, a young evangelist named Bob Pierce had been preaching in crusades throughout the Korean peninsula. During a break one afternoon, he visited an orphanage and was confronted by the woman in charge, who thrust a small child into his arms. "It's great that you're here telling people about faith, but what are you going to do for this little one?" she asked. Bob pulled a five-dollar bill from his pocket and then asked the woman, "How long will this last?"

"About one month," she replied. "When you get home, please continue to help us!"

Bob Pierce went back home, and the woman's idea of child sponsorship inspired people by the thousands to ensure a child's food, clothing, health, and education for just a few dollars each month.

At the potluck, Bob Seiple talked about the growth of that

vision, and his story scratched my curiosity. Sonya and I had the opportunity to drive him back to his hotel, and there we had a chance to visit. We were drawn to him immediately. Not only had Bob served in Vietnam, he flew the same kinds of missions I had in the A-6 Intruder. Bob had been stationed in Danang for thirteen months as a Marine Corps bombardier/navigator and like me had come home from the war without his best friend. And now as president of World Vision, one of his key areas of interest was reconciliation. We did indeed have much to talk about.

Toward the end of our brief conversation, he said, "We need someone to partner with Chet in San Francisco to help raise the money that literally primes the pump in villages and countries whose fields and hope have run dry. Would you be interested in looking at it?"

I told him I would. I told him that my personal brokenness related to Vietnam had prompted a growing compassion for others whose lives were in need of healing. I said I didn't know where it was leading, but I suspected our meeting was no coincidence.

Neither was a quote I had read in World Vision's magazine that Bob's office had sent me. It was by Joni Eareckson Tada, who had been disabled in a swimming accident and had started her own ministry to help others suffering from similar circumstances. She said, "If evangelism is taking the good news of the help to the helpless and hope to the hopeless, shouldn't we be most concerned with those who are the most helpless and the most hopeless?" And my perspective about World Vision immediately shifted.

Following a visit to World Vision's headquarters and a number of fact-finding meetings and interviews, I was offered the job. I stepped back and thought: Could I make a commitment, when I still had doubts about my future direction? Could I give up the freedom I'd enjoyed in private enterprise as an entrepreneur in a small team environment for a role in a large Christian organization?

And what about Sonya? What were her concerns? I thought she would be focused primarily on financial security since the offered salary was substantially less than I'd made my last year in the Navy eight years earlier. However, Glenn Murray, a respected friend, suggested Sonya sit down and share her thoughts with a small group of men I met with weekly. Without me there to interfere, or interpret, she might be able to speak freely to some guys I trusted and who cared for her.

This is exactly what happened. I learned that Sonya was very committed to follow me almost anywhere as long as she wasn't left behind, emotionally, and as long as she didn't have to fulfill someone else's expectations in supporting my new position.

When I accepted the position that August, I jumped in with the same energy with which I had approached my previous two careers. In three months I raced around the northern part of the Bay Area leaving a trail of coffee coasters and gas receipts in my pursuit of relationships and funding from the 250 major donors that were now my responsibility. I didn't stop until Christmas Eve, when I fell asleep in the recliner holding a cup of eggnog. It was really just a breather on the eve of a much longer trek.

One morning in February, Bob Seiple's assistant phoned and said, "Bob needs to fly to Southeast Asia in April to meet with our leadership team in the region, and he needs to visit with government officials in Hanoi. Would you be interested in joining him?"

It didn't take me five seconds to say yes.

Before I had even seen an itinerary, I knew what awaited me.

Gia Lam twice

Bangkok was our first stop, and after a day of meetings with World Vision's director for the Southeast Asia region, we were on our way to Hanoi courtesy of Vietnam Airlines. The vibrant countryside I saw passing by outside my window was not the beleaguered vestige of war I remembered from air strike maps and news reports. On our way to Hanoi, the narrow ribbon of crumbling roadway drew parallel to a railroad line. I could feel my pulse quicken. Dead ahead was a railroad station looming out of the afternoon haze.

There it was.

A freshly painted sign with bright led letters identified the entrance as the Gia Lam railroad yard. I asked the driver to stop. I got out and, slowly, walked over to the gate.

Though I had never set foot on this ground, I knew exactly where I was. I was standing in the crosshairs of an A-6 Navy jet on October 11, 1972, one of a dozen planes prepared to do its day's work. And it all came back. . . .

How I had depressed the red release button on the control stick. How my plane shuddered as our twenty-two bombs rippled off the wing stations on their free-fall. How I snatched the stick right back into my lap and pulled out of the dive.

As the nose came up on the horizon, I banked sharply left and added full power to avoid flying through the barrage of ground fire. I twisted upwards and sideways until I saw it, the Gia Lam railroad yard, roasting in a cloud of thick, black smoke.

Here I was, standing in front of a place that I had helped destroy many years earlier, on the same day Shannon was born. There was more to see. On a brief visit to the war museum the next morning, I saw the Hanoi I remembered. I saw glass cases stacked with U.S. aviators' helmets and uniforms. Memorabilia that belonged to names on a granite wall in another capital city. The twisted and scorched segments of American combat aircraft stacked in the outside courtyard, surrounded by North Vietnamese anti-aircraft artillery and missiles, turned my blood cold. I had processed much of this prior to the trip, but the irreverent display before me sucked the air out of me and filled me with the futility of the cost our country and our people had paid. Tears stung my eyes as I quietly headed for the car.

That afternoon, we met with the Vietnamese Minister of Health, who ended our meeting by asking us to consider helping a hundred disabled children living in the Thuy An Orphanage, forty miles west of Hanoi. We went to visit them the next day. Although a number of the children were relatively healthy and energetic, many others were ravaged by the effects of polio. Others could not speak or hear. By mid-afternoon, our visit was almost over, and I thought I had seen enough.

As we walked toward the stucco barracks at the rear of the compound, our World Vision doctor said, "This will be difficult. The kids we'll see now don't have much of a future."

I stepped carefully across a ceramic-tiled porch and slipped through a doorway into a dim room. As my eyes adjusted, I could see three girls sitting on a wood-slatted bed without a mattress. They were the poorest of the poor. Impaired mentally and physically, they rocked back and forth, silently and slowly clutching themselves with their pencil-thin arms.

When they saw me enter the room, a look of fear covered their tiny faces. Something inside me told me to wait. I eased across the colorless room and sat down on the far end of the bed where they huddled together. I softly stroked the shoulders of the two youngest girls closest to me, and they peered at me intently. Then, I moved gingerly to the other end of the bed and sat next to the oldest. She was the most disfigured of the three, and not a pretty child. Saliva streamed down her chin, and her eyes focused in different directions. "Do I dare reach out and try to touch her?" I thought.

Ever so gently I stretched out my hand on the bed. At that moment, the room was so still I could feel my pulse. Tears filled my eyes.

Astonishingly, this little girl slowly uncurled her contorted little arms, then reached toward me. My heart pounded, as she placed her twisted hand in mine. I felt the clutching of her tiny fingers in my palm.

I closed my eyes. I was stunned. I had come to comfort her, but she had comforted me.

This spindly, forgotten child reached out and, bravely, bridged our separateness.

In that moment, I realized we were both alike.

Alone. Struggling. And in need of each other.

In that room, in that orphanage, in a country I had once despised and was now seeking to embrace, I found what I'd really been looking for all along.

It had been waiting for me all these years.

Not in an airplane.

Or in a dream home.

Or in a title.

This small girl, who seemingly had nothing to offer, showed me that I didn't need all the answers. But I did need to be available to others.

My willingness to be present in the dark and difficult places of another was more important than my performance.

I thanked God for what He had taught me through a child. In her courage to reach beyond her fear and connect with me, she had given me the ultimate gift, the gift of freedom to love and to be loved.

9

Drawing a New Perspective

The object of drawing is not only to show what you are trying to portray, but also to show you. Paradoxically, the more clearly you can perceive and draw what you see in the external world, the more clearly the viewer can see you, and the more you can know about yourself.

—BETTY EDWARDS,
DRAWING ON THE RIGHT SIDE OF THE BRAIN[1]

It wasn't exactly the most romantic restaurant. Looking back, we could have certainly used the ambience.

On a tired Friday evening, Sonya and I, and another couple who had been friends for several years, settled back in our chairs. We studied the large, laminated menus and had a hard time making up our minds. We finally came to a consensus: The four mud-encrusted bulldozers parked right outside our window did not qualify as "view dining."

During dessert, the topic of relationships came up. The four of us began to exchange legendary lowlights from our marriages. I told about my years in flight school and that when it came to missing dinners, I had posted more consistent late arrivals than

Chicago's O'Hare International Airport. One night after staying out late with an exchange pilot from Britain's Royal Air Force, I came home to a cold shoulder in bed. My squadron buddy came home to a dark house and a surprise: His wife had nailed his dinner steak to the door!

Sonya usually laughed at this story. Her reserved smile told me what I already knew. After twenty-four years of marriage, we were still trying to define our life together as empty nesters. Jeff and Shannon were both away at college. Even with frequent opportunities to be together, the family was experiencing a permanent shift in the context of our relationship. Our daily routine at home hadn't slowed down much, and we were still trying to adjust to a life no longer focused on our children but on wondering what it meant to relate to each other for the first time in eons.

Talk at the restaurant picked up at dessert when our friends asked Sonya how she was doing with my new ministry. She looked abruptly at me, then back at our friends, and said, "I love Jim, but I'm not sure I'm going to be able to live with him anymore."

The words felt like someone had just poured ice water down the back of my neck. It certainly doused the conversation. While our friends wanted to dissect her comment, Sonya teared up. She had gone as far as she intended. And based on what she had said, I knew there would be no dancing after dinner.

I couldn't think of anything constructive to say on the short drive home. As we were getting in bed, I turned to Sonya and said, "I know you weren't joking tonight, and I'm making the assumption that you were serious about what you said." She still didn't want to discuss it. Yet, I knew we needed to talk.

The next day I kept a prior commitment to attend a San Francisco Giants baseball game with friends. In between pitches and too many home run trots by the visiting team, I had plenty of time to think about Sonya's comment. I knew our marriage had improved in the past few years, but this was a new twist. I felt that we had put much of our past behind us, when I had been AWOL, mentally as well as physically, for much of the time. We had survived the "gone years." I was always gone to flight school, gone to air shows, gone to be the best. But since repeating our marriage vows and trying to make time for each other, I felt we were doing better. In fact, I thought we had done a reasonable job of adjusting to the kids being away.

Sonya's restaurant remark, however, made it painfully clear that we weren't nearly as far along as I thought. She obviously still wasn't getting her deeper needs met, and I was missing some major signals. I knew she had a desire for greater intimacy, and although I wanted the same thing, we weren't experiencing it in our relationship as much as we both needed.

We were living in different worlds, and I still hadn't grasped it. My work with World Vision was energizing and full of variety. Her days were spent in the bank, working eight to five and coming home exhausted and frustrated, then fixing dinner.

I was traveling the world; she was fighting freeway gridlock.

I regularly spoke to appreciative crowds; she dealt daily with irate customers.

I could set my own schedule; she was tied to a vault's time clock.

Even before Sonya made her comment at dinner, I realized we were struggling to find common ground. Why was this so hard for us? After Cannon Beach, after renewing our vows, after reconciling the pain of lost friends and the war, after nearly eight years of faith and fellowship through our local church, by any measure, our marriage should have been thriving.

What did my words at the altar really mean?

"For better, for worse, for richer, for poorer, in sickness and in health, to love and to cherish. . . ." The only thing I could come up with was that I had more questions than answers.

A day later, on Saturday afternoon, I was resting on the couch while Sonya was running errands and buying groceries. The question occurred to me, "So Jim, how much cherishing have you done lately?" I knew immediately that if we were still dating in college, I certainly wouldn't be lying around waiting for her to come by the apartment and fix dinner.

The vacuum and dusting came first.

A shave and shower came next.

Flowers and a nicely set dinner table followed.

When Sonya came home, I greeted her with a kiss, a hug, and a special meal at Chez Horsley. Together, all of these things sent a long-overdue message that I did love her, and that I wanted her to know it.

Maybe I had learned a few things after all. Her warm response and tender smile told me that we weren't completely derailed. But I needed to put a whole lot more "cherish" back in the equation if we were going to stay on track.

Some of our circumstances had changed, but some had not. I still raced down the freeway like I was late for an air show, I still kept loading my agenda, and I still liked to win arguments.

Complacency, not irritations, was our worst threat. We knew we had to stay focused on accepting our differences, and we understood that we needed to be careful in our expectations of one another.

I knew I was beginning to change, and that if I wasn't yet the most understanding husband, at least I was trying to be the hardest-working one. Our prior counseling had helped. I was experiencing some peace and feeling some intimacy. I had defused some restlessness, and my visit to the orphanage in Hanoi had provided some direction. The real balancing act was making sure my work, which energized me greatly, didn't throw me off track in my commitment with Sonya. I needed the balance because I knew that none of my time alone at work would matter if Sonya and I couldn't find peace in our marriage, together. Sonya needed to restore her identity, and I needed to support and encourage her in the process. She had contributed all she could as the dutiful wife, and she wasn't going to live in my shadow any longer. And I agreed.

Our faith was beginning to play a major difference in our ability to grow our marriage. In spite of our difficulties, we could always come back to a core belief that would transcend our human frailties. Looking back, our faith was, in many cases, all that held us together. But it wasn't easy.

I was still learning the basics of lifting the visor on my emotions and finding the freedom to be as vulnerable as I needed to be. Yet in our church environment, it was a natural tendency for me to portray a guy who had everything in his life pretty much together. After all, I had been a Blue Angel and a successful real estate developer, and was now a leader in a major Christian ministry.

We showed up on Sundays wearing our smiles, and I would talk about how great we were doing. But inside, on more days than I care to count, I was struggling. I could say all the right words, and in my heart I believed and tried to live them. In reality, I still wanted to control my circumstances. God wanted me to rely on *His* power, not fix things on my own. The resources were there, all I had to do was find the Source. It wasn't much different than buying a new chain saw then wondering why I was having trouble cutting down trees when, in fact, I hadn't started the motor.

I had reached a point in life of feeling both buoyed and baffled. I had worked through so much, and yet there was so much work I still had to do. I had just begun to feel some of life's losses, and yet feeling the grief had brought some real healing. The biggest paradox greeted me every day when I looked in the mirror to shave. I didn't know how I could be so responsive dealing with problems in aviation or business and yet so resistant in responding to relationships.

I couldn't see it. I only knew how to look at life one way, and that was to accomplish a task in the most efficient, smartest, best way possible. Relationships, particularly marriage, didn't fit my template for success. I wanted to achieve something good with Sonya, with Jeff and Shannon, with my dad. I wanted these relationships to be the best they could, but sometimes the work required felt so uncomfortable.

That's when I knew there was hope. I had been uncomfortable many times before, and had learned something about being in relationships that felt so up in the air. . . .

Living upside down

With the Blue Angels, we used to pride ourselves on our pursuit of the ultimate in perfection while performing outside our comfort zone. Nothing had been as discomforting, or as potentially hazardous, as our Double Farvel. The maneuver originated with the Blues in 1979 with Bruce Davey flying slot. Mike Nord enhanced the technique in 1980 when he moved into the slot and I joined the team as the left wingman. The precedent was set for each succeeding slot pilot to do what he could to improve the formation.

The first time I saw the maneuver from the ground, I was stunned. The flight leader and the slot pilot were flying upside down, the two wingmen were right side up, and all of them were within a sleeve length of each other as they roared down the flight line in level flight at 350 knots, three hundred feet off the ground.

My second year with the Blues gave me a shot at refining this upside down wonder. My first official practice opportunity started at a safe distance above the ground but low enough to have a clear horizon. I established a position one hundred feet behind the Boss and slightly offset above and to the right.

"Rolling in," called the Boss, and the nose of his A-4 lifted slightly. Then the jet abruptly rolled to the inverted position, and the Boss "set" the attitude at level flight by pushing the stick forward.

"Stabilized level, Nag. Cleared in."

And I attempted to replicate the Boss's roll to inverted. Flopping upside down was the easy part. Lining my aircraft up on the Boss's plane was hilarious. I jerked around like a fish yanked onto the pier before our safety observer, Tim Dineen, gave me an advisory call: "You got all those snakes killed in the cockpit yet?"

Very funny. And I rolled upright, then tried it again. Gradually I began to grasp the picture. I had to completely ignore the ground horizon for my orientation, and focus solely on the Boss. If I could lock everything else out of my vision, then his aircraft became my horizon. It wouldn't make any difference what attitude he was in, and I could stay locked on. After a couple more practice sessions, we were rolling in simultaneously with only twenty feet or so between us, and within a second or so I could stabilize directly behind and slightly above him. Nothing felt comfortable at first. The stick movements were different, my vantage point was different, and the safety "clear" areas were different. Every time I took my gaze off the Boss, I immediately lost my bearings, but if I stayed focused with the right perspective, it worked. Getting out of the formation was just about as much fun as getting into it!

Learning to fly inverted in formation was an important lesson about what could be accomplished if I would open my mind to a new viewpoint and put some effort into adjusting to it. It entailed the willingness to realize that there were other ways of looking at something. The payoff came in being able to do something beyond my expectations of comfort in a way I never would have thought possible.

If I could fly with a new perspective in an airplane, why couldn't I do the same in relationships? Why couldn't I focus on the person—be it my wife, my child, my parent, my friend—and not the distractions?

If the Double Farvel was the graphic example of this freeing possibility, then all I needed was a personal illustration. . . .

Meeting Dad for the first time

I had always enjoyed sketching when I was younger. In high school it had been sports figures, in flight training it had been airplanes, and since Vietnam, it had been nothing, because I had not drawn in years.

Following the World Vision trip to Hanoi, I picked up an intriguing book whose title I couldn't resist, *Drawing on the Right Side of the Brain*. I brought it home, and after completing a few of the opening exercises, I succumbed to the author's next intriguing assignment. I was to draw the picture of an elderly man carving three wood ducks by looking at it upside down!

Talk about a changed perspective. Following some simple instructions about drawing what I saw, I went at it, hardly believing that the result would resemble the picture. In fact, I almost felt like apologizing to the man in the scene, for how contorted he would look if I finished it. I felt for the ducks, too, because they would probably end up looking like bowling pins.

After thirty minutes I still wasn't sure what I had. Even when I put my pencil down, I squirmed. All I could see were shapes that matched the confusing upside-down picture in the book. I turned my page right side up, and I was amazed at what I had done. I showed it to Sonya. "That's fantastic. How did you do that?" she asked.

"I just followed the directions," I said. The book's author, Betty Edwards, said that people see what their mind tells them, not what the picture actually looks like. Turning the picture upside down caused me to lose my cues, until all I had were the exact shapes and lines interrelated in one big whole.

Drawing an image turned upside down prevented me from drawing what my memory told me something ought to look like. All the old reference points disappeared, and I had to concentrate completely on the reality of what I was seeing, then repeat each line and shape. The lesson about trying to see things as they really are stayed with me. As important as that principle is in drawing, I had an opportunity to find that it had broader applications.

At a weekend couples retreat, I listened intently as Dr. Howard Hendricks, a noted Christian lecturer and teacher, said, "If our faith doesn't work at home, don't export it." It was more than a tad convicting. I knew I had a family relationship that needed some healing—and the benefit of a changed perspective.

For too many years, my perspective of Dad had been one of a father whose alcoholism had injected a pain into our family that hadn't been healed. The unpredictability of his behavior and the harsh, painful comments he could make were all spawned by his drinking and induced the distance and tension I felt in our relationship. Before I left home in Billings for college, I rarely saw Dad unable to function because of the booze. In reality, it occasionally took a lot of discernment to determine what shape he was in when he got home. And I developed a keen ability to sniff out what to expect when we sat down for dinner.

He hadn't always been that way. He had attended college and a variety of Navy midshipmen training courses on the East Coast before marrying my mother in 1945. Mom hadn't been concerned with his social drinking while they were dating, and assumed he'd grow out of it when they started to have a family.

He never stopped. But it never stopped him either. Dad had a sharp mind and an infectious sense of humor, and everyone liked him. He was an exceptionally gifted, competitive athlete in football and basketball, and Mom never remembers a time when he wasn't available in a crisis.

That changed in 1964 when I left home for college. Over the next nine years his drinking increased, and his reliability at home and at work deteriorated. Mom divorced him in 1973 and moved to Denver to be closer to my sister, Nancy, and her husband. Dad spent the next fourteen years trying to get a grip on his life. A heart attack in Redding in 1988 nearly ended it, and a year later we found ourselves together on a literal trip down memory lane.

My grandparents had moved into a nursing home in Logan, Utah, and Dad and I had rendezvoused in Salt Lake to drive north in a rental car to see them. Following a day with his parents, we continued north to Soda Springs, and spent a day with Dad's brothers and friends from the old days. The drive was easy, but our conversation was miserable. Along the way, I made it a point to drive by every home and each school I had attended from the time I was born until moving from Logan to Billings when I entered high school. I had imagined them all so differently than what I found. When I saw them, again, after such a long time, they all seemed so small and distorted. I was beginning to feel the same way about some of my reactions and feelings toward Dad.

Initially, it wasn't reconciliation as much as it was a restoration of peace. We began to find opportunities to visit, and even though I was wary about whether he was still drinking or not, I felt free of any burden of having to be responsible for his behavior. I had emotionally processed much of our history, and I was looking for peace instead of a battlefront. It was hit or miss for the next five years. Some visits were tough, others were surprising. On a more recent occasion, I had stopped in Boise to see Dad and my grandmother, who had moved into a nursing home there after my grandfather died. Every one of the elderly people we saw lit up when they saw Dad, and he had a kind word and a warm touch for each of them. The thought occurred to me that I spent a lot of time speaking about touching the lives of others. Dad was actually *doing* it. People loved him for it. Their joy was my cue to view him in a way I never had before.

Around the time Sonya and I had moved to Seattle as part of World Vision's headquarters relocation, Dad flew to Seattle for a mini family reunion with his two brothers and a sister who lived on Bainbridge Island. Sonya had left for Grants Pass, Oregon, to spend time with her mom, who was suffering from cancer. Following the Saturday activities with his siblings, Dad and I attended church on Sunday. On our way to the airport, we stopped for breakfast and had a chance to talk. I resolved that I wanted our time together to be better than it had been on our previous visits.

Looking at Dad as we sat in the restaurant, I saw two different men. In my mind I saw the memories of a father who seemed so distant. But other images emerged, pictures of overnight camping trips, good times at sporting events, golf outings with friends, laughter that engulfed us, and family drives on the weekend.

As I ignored the history and concentrated on the present, I also saw another man, a tired, aging father in his mid-seventies who loved his children as much as he knew how. A man whose youth had been full of hopes and dreams—some realized, many lost. My mind recalled the lesson I'd learned from drawing, and I continued to focus on Dad not as I remembered him but as he really was. And with that perspective, I saw that he was, in the very best sense of the word, my father.

In his eyes I could see regrets, things he wished he could have done over and things he preferred to forget. And I'm sure I mirrored the same reflection for him in the things I'd failed to do and say, and the things I wish I hadn't.

I asked him, "Did the message this morning about forgiveness make any sense?" He acknowledged that it had, and that it wasn't the first time he had heard something on the subject. He had begun to attend a small community church in Boise and was beginning to feel comfortable with it.

"Dad, I need to ask for your forgiveness for all that I've done, and left undone. I hope you understand that you don't need to ask for forgiveness from Scott, Nancy, or me. As far as we're concerned—as far as I'm concerned—you're forgiven and loved by us all."

He nodded, but I could tell he didn't know what to say.

"Dad, what would it take for you to be able to forgive yourself?"

He grasped the concept, but I'm not sure he believed it. In his mind, he still seemed unable to shake the idea that somehow he needed to work his way back to God, to earn the grace that was free for the taking. We talked about God's unconditional acceptance and forgiveness, and I said, "You can put the weight down. No one's asking or expecting you to carry anything."

I wanted to take his misperception of God away and substitute it with the "upside-down" reality of a Jesus who died so that he could live. However, I knew if I pushed it on him, it wouldn't be grace. What could I do?

I could accept him.

I could be for him the kind of person I hoped Jeff and Shannon would be for me.

I could obey by doing the right and good thing. I could honor my father.

I could see him as the person he was and offer him the ultimate gift someone had given me: I could finally love him unconditionally.

When I dropped him off at the airport, I gave him a long hug and told him I loved him. It had been too long. I had found a new perspective on relationships—and myself.

Nothing left unsaid

At the same time, 350 miles south in Grant's Pass, Oregon, Sonya was visiting her mom, now battling cancer in her kidney, liver, and lungs. Three months after the doctors found it, a tumor in her liver had begun to grow at an alarming rate. Sonya, Jeff, Shannon, and I had spent Christmas with her, and while the time together couldn't have gone much better, a rude, uninvited guest had entered our lives.

Memorial Day was approaching, and Sonya wanted to spend the long weekend with her mom. She wanted to deepen her relationship with a mother she hadn't known as well as she wanted, and time was growing short. Sonya was the youngest of three children, following her oldest sister, Suzanne, by eight years and her brother, Gary, by ten. More than once she had heard her parents refer to her as "our little accident."

She had enjoyed the adventure and felt the demands of growing up on her parents' ranch in Enterprise, Oregon. Her father, while good-humored, worked long hours; her mom valued discipline more than fun. Sonya learned obedience from her parents at the cost of doing without some of the warmth that would have been so welcome, particularly from her mom.

Cancer put a whole new set of issues on the table. Early in the process, the disease prompted Sevilla to tighten her resolve that she could deal with this too. She could fight this thing on her own, thank you. But by May, she was losing the battle. Her Christian faith in God was solid, but she was nervous about the pain she had been told to expect. As Sonya and I drove down from Seattle, we didn't know if she had a matter of days or weeks to live. I wondered if Sonya would be able to find a way to talk to her mom about the things that had gone unsaid for so many years.

"If we do nothing else," I said to her, "let's not come home with anything left unsaid." Sonya agreed. For the last hundred miles, she thought about what she might say—and what it would mean.

We arrived on Friday. Jeff and Shannon were driving up from Northern California and would arrive on Saturday. When we walked in the door, Sevilla was pleased to see us but looked pale and weak. She slumped in her recliner. Her breathing was assisted by an oxygen machine. Our visit that evening was short and difficult, and we went to bed in a state of exhaustion. The next morning, Sonya's mom had more strength, and before the kids arrived, the three of us sat in her sunroom and talked quietly. Then I slipped out to the recliner on the patio to give Sonya the opportunity I knew she wanted.

I tried to read a grocery store novel, but I couldn't turn the pages. A much bigger story was being written in the next room. A mother and daughter were talking in a way I had never heard before. Their voices were tender, their silences long.

"Let's be as honest as we can with each other, Mom. . . ."

There were stories, and questions, and more than once, there were tears.

"We don't know how much time we have, do we?" Sonya said. At that point, she began rubbing her mom's hands and feet with lotion.

"I'm so grateful that you're here," said Sevilla.

Later that morning, she asked me to come sit by her couch. By now she was very tired. Words were at a luxury, and she spoke more with her eyes.

"Jim, I hope you know how much our family appreciates you."

No longer was she the mother-in-law; she was talking to a son. She looked up and mouthed the words, "I . . . love . . . you."

In the past, we had experienced some differences, but on this day, I made sure I told her exactly how I felt. "I love *you.*"

So did our kids. Their attentiveness and tenderness was a comfort and a joy to their grandmother, and Sonya and I were grateful they could share their heart-felt love.

The next morning after breakfast, Sonya's brother and sister and their families gathered with us on the patio. We circled around her mom, who wanted to stand but could not. We joined hands, and I prayed. I gave thanks for the blessing of having the weekend together and for the love and joy that had filled Sevilla's home. I offered thanks for what Sonya's mom had meant to our family, and I prayed that God would continue to give her the same love, comfort, and peace she had found over the weekend. God was in our midst, and our small circle of family was closer than it had ever been before. Reluctant to leave, we said our good-byes with more than prolonged hugs.

The first week of June I flew to Colorado Springs to attend the graduation of a special young man who was graduating as an officer in the United States Air Force.

Second Lieutenant Tad Clark.

From where I sat, he looked relieved, proud, and glad to be on his way to flight training in Wichita Falls, Texas. After the ceremony I found Tad and Tonya in the crowd, and said, "There's only one person who's prouder than us—and I know he's looking on."

Sonya had gone back to Grant's Pass. Her mother was barely alert now, and Sonya was committed to stay for as long as she was needed. She chose to sleep in her mom's bedroom while her mom rested next to her on a hospital bed. In the middle of the night on June 10, Sonya awoke with a start and got up to check on her mom. Silently and painlessly, Sevilla had breathed her last just moments before. Sonya knelt down next to her mother and said good-bye with a whisper and a kiss. And then called me in tears.

Her mom was gone. Yet in the midst of her pain, Sonya took great comfort in the relationship she and her mom had built. She knew she and her mom had said everything they needed to share, words of understanding, forgiveness, and a mutual love. Words that described the depth of relationship she valued.

Through her strength and courage in such difficult circumstances, Sonya had modeled what love looked like in relationships. In the midst of her giving, I had come to appreciate, even more, the woman I had married.

10

A Vision for Life

"Compassion is the courage to care outside your comfort zone."

—JIM HORSLEY

I was slowly waking up to the reality of real intimacy in my marriage. I still felt tremendously awake in my work. Though I no longer snapped to life at five o'clock with a fighter pilot's breakfast of coffee and a cigar, I felt alive to the moment. I was energized and engaged with the people I met. Keeping up with them had never been an issue, until I had the great fortune of encountering a man named Dave Dornsife.

Racing with mosquitoes

I first met him at his office in Pleasanton, California, in the early 1990s. Dave Dornsife had blond hair and stood six feet three inches tall. A former football player and shot-putter on the University of Southern California track team, he now competed internationally in the construction arena. He was bright, good looking, and had a terrific sense of humor. His toughness in business belied his softness for people, and his heart for the poor fired his commitment to provide something of lasting value with his time and his resources. His first major gift was part of his family's foundation contribution to our World Vision's water program in the African country of Malawi.

One of the best parts of my job as a development officer was to take friends to see World Vision's projects so they could get a first-person look at how their involvement was making a difference. Before I could book the flight, Dave called me one day and said, "I need to visit the project to see how it's doing. When do we make the trip?"

A thirteen-hour flight from San Francisco via New York landed us in Senegal on Africa's West Coast. Three days in the desert visiting our water program gave Dave some perspective on well drilling, and we reboarded Air Afrique for our cross-continent trip to Malawi. After stops in Mali and Abidjan in 100-degree heat, we felt like we were riding a pogo stick before arriving in Lome, Togo, in late afternoon. Since our next flight wasn't until ten o'clock that evening, we squeezed in a quick taxi tour and short rest at a local hotel before heading back to the airport. By midnight, our Ethiopian Air connection still hadn't arrived. When the uniformed security people locked the doors to the waiting room and turned out the lights, we looked for anyone who could tell us what was going on. Unfortunately, we didn't speak the native language, so we reluctantly stretched out on two dilapidated plastic couches.

There were advantages to our accommodations. At two o'clock that morning, we heard our jet taxi in and were first in line at the gate. The only ones to beat us to the plane were the mosquitoes. It took short stops in Zaire, Kenya, and Zambia and two more changes in airlines to reach Llongwe, Malawi. As we dragged our bags to a taxi, Dave strongly suggested I not quit my day job to become a tour director.

The next day we boarded a van with our World Vision project manager and headed up the road into the jungle. When the road ran out, we hiked through hip-high grass to a clearing, where local elders welcomed us with wide smiles and handshakes. One of them explained the piped water project Dave's foundation had funded. To take advantage of a spring at the top of the hill, villagers had installed an outlet and piped the water down to a newly built cement holding tank. They then dug over thirty miles of trench for the PVC pipe that would provide fresh, clean water to the cluster of villages in the region.

The people were thrilled, and so was Dave. No longer would thousands of people in the region need to drink contaminated standing water. The visit primed Dave's enthusiasm for finding other opportunities to help. When we returned home, I submitted another foundation proposal, this one for the funding of a drilling rig in Senegal. The grant was approved, and the rig was purchased and assembled. A few months later, Dave and I were headed back to Senegal, and our daughters came with us. Dave's daughter, Rhonda, was a nurse and wanted to get a look at our health programs. For Shannon, it was her UCLA graduation present, and I was thrilled she was with me.

Three hours of swirling sand and backbreaking road brought us to the edge of a thatch-roofed village. The landscape was barren, but even with the windows rolled up, we could hear the celebration. Stepping from our jeep we were engulfed by villagers. Drums and music pounded our ears as we walked into the throngs of dancing women. Water was gushing out of the ground like a geyser, and the people were ecstatic. For the first time in decades, their village would have clean water, and their children could enjoy good health. I had never in my life seen so many people so grateful for a gift.

Dave and I wept with our daughters at the joy we shared as we posed for a photo in the spray from the water. But we didn't need a picture to be convinced of the project's staggering impact. It had only taken three days and two hundred feet of drilling to tap into Senegal's huge aquifer, providing a new, permanent well for upwards of six hundred villagers. Over the course of a year, fifty new wells would bring water to thirty thousand people. Over the course of ten years, three hundred thousand people would experience a vastly improved quality of life because of Dave Dornsife.

As a bottom-line guy, he loved measurable results. He took great pride and ownership in a project he could invest in and direct. One night at dinner I challenged him to think beyond the numbers, and the other definable outcomes within his grasp. I knew Dave's heart. I knew he rooted his faith in the same God I served. I knew about other desperate regions in Africa that couldn't measure hope with a cup because their needs couldn't be solved in three days, or three months, or even three years. While I appreciated Dave's generosity, I wanted to test the waters.

"Suppose the need didn't fit a tight timeline," I asked. "What if the results were really out of our hands."

"Keep going. I'm with you," he said.

"How deep are you willing to plant, and how long are you willing to wait, for God to provide the increase?"

"That's a great question," said Dave. "What do you have in mind?"

Our programs in the Islamic Republic of Mauritania were next on our trip agenda. I pulled out a map of this West African country trying to survive in the sand dunes, and gave Dave a thumbnail history. The culture was similar to Senegal's—Muslim, Arabic, and French speaking. For years, the encroaching desert had forced nomads to settle in the southern regions. Out of the dust, Nouakchott, the capital city, had grown from a handful of wanderers to about seven hundred thousand inhabitants. These former nomads and herdsmen lived in scrap metal hovels. They had no education or marketable skills. With so many sick children and limited futures, the main industry was despair.

I explained to Dave that World Vision had been working with the people since re-entering the country after the Gulf War. Within the past year, a literacy program had been envisioned that could give children and adults an opportunity they had never had to learn to read. Reading could seed education, and education could help people harvest new skills with small micro-enterprise loans needed to start businesses, which could then create the products and services that could infuse hope and provide some improvement in the people's overall quality of life.

"It won't happen overnight," I said. "It's going to take time. But what's three to five years when you're talking about changing an entire generation?"

Dave wanted to know more. Two days later we headed north by Land Rover, a harrowing transit across the Senegal River and endless miles of barren sand to Nouakchott. On a scorching morning, we sat with our daughters in one of the city's dimly lit classrooms and watched fathers and mothers, farmers, and children holding their Ping Pong paddle-sized chalkboards learning how to read. The commitment and capacity of our staff and those few hours with the people were enough to convince Dave that he needed to be involved. He wanted to be a part of the literacy program, whose dividends, in the form of changed lives, would keep on growing for years.

Our visit that day gave me time to reflect on the gentleman who now joined me on the other side of the world. My relationship with Dave wasn't about fundraising but rather a deep mutual trust and friendship that grew over time. We had backpacked, hiked, and traveled the world together, and my times with him were always treasured. Well, *almost* always. One night during a return visit to Mauritania, we found ourselves on the backside of the desert, the guests of a modern-day sheik. His castle was a canvas tent, complete with exotic Arabian rugs and lounging cushions. At the end of our evening meal, as a gesture of great hospitality, our host invited us to sit with him and enjoy a ceremonial swallow of fresh camel's milk. This creamy elixir filled a quart-sized jar, and I nervously prepared myself to take a tiny, polite swig.

"You need to know something," Dave told our host. "Jim, here, told me he loves this stuff so much that he wants to drink my share."

The Muslim smiled and handed me the milk.

I grinned weakly at Dave, knowing that common courtesy, along with the Old Testament admonition of "Thou shalt not kill," now obligated me to drink the yellowish, warm whey. I made sure I smiled after taking a healthy gulp and handed the jar back. I thanked our host. Then, not wanting to risk any more adventure, Dave and I took our bed pads and walked to the top of the dune to sleep under the stars.

The next day as we approached the outskirts of Nouakchott in our vehicle, I felt sicker than at any time in my life. I begged for death so that I'd feel better. For some reason, God chose not to answer my prayer.

Understanding a rationale for contributing to a literacy program in the remoteness of Africa wasn't easy. But over several trips, Dave developed an enormous sense of affinity and compassion for those who badly needed help. He didn't do it for the self-gratification, although the tremendous sense of fulfillment he got from being a part of the drilling rig project in Senegal surely filled his cup. He certainly didn't feel obligated or coerced. And I could tell from the sincere dignity and respect he showed the villagers that his giving hadn't been primed by sympathy or pity.

I really believe Dave Dornsife gave to the projects in Africa for another reason, one that he may not have even realized. He gave, I'm convinced, because his need to give to something bigger than himself was as great as the needs of others he encountered in his travels. When he looked into the eyes of a young boy who would grow up and might not be able to read a book, or write his own name, Dave's questions of "How long will this take to be successful?" and "When will we see some measurable results?" faded away. At that moment, God's impulse convinced him that one boy's future outweighed one man's need to be in control.

And because Dave's heart went out to one child, he was able, through his compassion and his financial resources, to touch the lives of hundreds more.

Dave experienced a major breakthrough. He found a way to give without experiencing anything in return. He looked forward to seeing positive results but no longer demanded them. He simply felt grateful to give to others a portion of his time and treasure God had intended for him to share all along.

Dave Dornsife's greatest gift, however, is what he has offered me without even thinking about it. Prior to my visit to North Vietnam and the orphanage in Hanoi, my life had been a banquet room filled with acquaintances. I could look out and see a crowd of smiling faces, but rarely did I know the real hopes and hurts of the individuals themselves. I had developed a number of close friends over the years, friends from the Navy and friends through my speaking. But my friendship with Dave broke the mold. He has helped me to see my world—*one person at a time.*

North to Seattle

In the spring of 1995, my landscape shifted again. This time was different. This time I wasn't pursuing opportunity, I was part of it. The opportunity belonged to World Vision. When the international relief organization, for which I now served as director of development, moved its headquarters from Southern California to Federal Way, Washington, near Seattle, Sonya and I eagerly headed north.

This time, I wasn't changing jobs and trying to convince Sonya to say yes, because for years we had wanted to be back in the Northwest. This time, we didn't begrudge the moving vans, we welcomed them right up to the curb of our townhouse in Pleasanton. The move was a first. Instead of showing up on different days, in different cars, we made the exodus together. There was a new division of labor. This time, Sonya picked out the carpet and colors, and I unloaded the boxes. Life was upside down, just the way I liked to fly it.

One thing hadn't changed, and that was our penchant for getting settled quickly. Boxes were unpacked and pictures hung within three days of getting in the front door. The mail hadn't even begun arriving before new routines fell into place and Sonya and I settled into our new suroundings.

We weren't California exports, we were coming back to our roots in the Pacific Northwest, and while I didn't claim to bring any sun with me, I knew I had come with a new attitude. Even though my fundraising duties took me around the country and on periodic international trips, I wanted my world to be larger than just World Vision's arena. I wanted to be part of the world I now called home by finding a way to get connected in the community. Within a year I was on the board of Seafair, Seattle's annual late-summer citywide water-theme block party. The committee was appreciative of my background as a former Blue Angel and what I could do to help the Seafair committee organize its yearly air show above Lake Washington.

Speaking opportunities started to surface, and I began to get acquainted with the citizens of Seattle. But it was an early morning meeting at a downtown athletic club that really opened the door.

An angel named Mary

A friend had invited me to attend his monthly breakfast group to listen to a presentation by a local Seattle businessman named Don Mowat. "As an entrepreneur," he began, "I'm accustomed to measuring the productivity and the worth of an endeavor in quantifiable terms such as sales, output, growth, and certainly, profits." For the next thirty minutes this soft-spoken, earnest gentleman thoroughly redefined this definition of success by relating a personal story that had me sitting up in my chair.

Don's story was about Bosnia, and how he and his wife, Molly, had traveled there for the first time. "Twenty-seven months ago," he said, "I was seeing on television and in magazines the faces of children and adults suffering the horrors of war. I became over-whelmed by the question 'How could this be occurring in this decade at the back door of Western Europe?' I asked myself, 'How can I respond?' "

Don told how a friend encouraged him to "simply go there." The man introduced him to Peter Kuzmic, a renowned Eastern European Protestant theologian, and Peter invited Don to go with him to Bosnia so he and his wife could see for themselves what they and the rest of the world couldn't believe was happening on their television screen, much less in real life.

Don then painted a stark, yet honest, picture of a country that was bleeding to death. Don described Bosnia as "a very beautiful Alpine-like land but at the same time a place of great darkness and very little hope." He ticked off the harsh statistics:

- 2,750,000 refugees, few of which had been allowed to return to their homes

- fifty-five thousand documented rapes, many occurring in the presence of husbands, children, and other family members

This was the backdrop to the pain of two hundred thirty thousand who had been killed, including sixty-five thousand children. The intangible wounds—hatred, unforgiveness, intimidation, and fear—were permanent and immeasurable. Don's story wasn't as much about numbers or bottomless sorrow as it was about a face-to-face encounter. It was about what he called "the gift of presence" he said he learned about during his first day in Bosnia.

"I was in a refugee feeding station run by Agape, the relief organization run by the seminary that Peter Kuzmic had founded in eastern Croatia. Standing next to me was a young woman I'll call Mary, who taught at the seminary. Together, we saw a line of wet and cold refugees file past silently to receive their one warm meal of the day. I watched an old man and a young boy receive their food and take their places at one of the two long wooden tables. I couldn't take my eyes off them.

"With Mary as my interpreter, I asked the director of the feeding station if he knew about the two. He said he did. The man had been separated from his wife and had no other family. The young boy's father had been killed, and the mother had been taken away to an unknown fate. Like the man, this boy now had no other family, and the two often ate together."

Don continued. "Our interpreter invited me to go receive food in the line and join the people. I sat next to the man and the boy, and Mary joined us. The two Bosnians began asking her about me, and she told them that I was simply there to observe and learn of their needs. I sat silently through my meal and was overwhelmed by the feeling of insufficiency to respond to the hopelessness I felt in that room."

Don then peeled back the meaning of the title of his speech, "The Gift of Your Presence." He related how Mary told him the story of her preceding three years in Bosnia. She had chosen to remain in the frequently shelled front-line city of Osijek in eastern Croatia because she wanted to be present for the elderly and children who took refuge in the seminary's basement.

"As we drove away from the feeding station, through the devastated front-line towns of Bosnia still smoldering from the artillery shellings of that morning, I told Mary how helpless I had felt to do or say anything meaningful to the man and the boy. 'I'm at a loss as to how to respond to all of this suffering,' I said.

"Mary simply replied, 'What your presence did for that man and boy at our meal today was give them hope. Just the idea that somebody cared, that somebody out there even knew that they were on this earth and not forgotten. That's what your presence meant to them. Your presence is a wonderful gift. Be satisfied with nothing more.'"

Don then paused, and in soft, measured words said to all of us in the room, "I challenge you, today, to find your own Bosnia, to take the risk and step out of your comfort zone of the familiar and into a place where maybe you have never ventured before with the purpose of simply being available and present. Available and present to those who are broken, those who mourn, who are powerless, who have little hope, and for whom nobody—nobody—cares.

"Molly and I have found that, at the intersection of our physical presence and the deep need of another, we find fulfillment and contentment, and yes, strangely enough, even joy. For that joy, I believe, is the sure sign of God's presence. Nothing that I have ever accomplished in business or acquired with the fruits of my endeavors can remotely compare to it, for it is a fulfillment that springs from being in accord with what I was designed for.

"May God richly bless you on your journey. Amen."

Everyone in the room applauded. Though I had never been to Bosnia, Don Mowat's story reflected the emotion and impact I had experienced in Hanoi and Africa. After his talk, I made my way forward to the podium and waited for the men huddled around him to end their discussion.

When it was my turn, I shook his hand and told him how much I appreciated his talk. I said, "I've experienced some of the same things you talked about this morning and would like to spend a few minutes with you if you've got the time." He said he would, and a few minutes later we found a quiet corner of the lobby to sit down and visit.

After visiting a bit about his talk, I briefly shared my Hanoi orphanage story with him. I told him, "Many of the men in that room this morning really identified with what you were saying. I would just like to encourage you to keep telling your story because it's a message that many of us need to keep hearing." We exchanged business cards, shook hands, and went our separate ways.

Late that afternoon my office phone rang, and it was Don. "I've been thinking about what you said earlier today, and I just wanted to call and say thanks for the encouragement. I've been wrestling with the interest that people might have in my message, and you have helped me clarify its importance."

I responded, "I feel we've arrived at a similar place. From different directions, we've come to the point of needing to respond to who God is in our life. And our response, as you experienced in Bosnia, has far less to do with being sufficient and capable as it does with being brought to a point of availability."

"I agree, Jim," replied Don. "I'd like to talk about this some more."

With that, our friendship began. The more time I spent with Don, the more I began to understand what it meant to be present in the life of another. I began to see how one person, even without saying a single word, could, simply through his or her presence, make a powerful difference in the life of others.

One day over lunch, I told Don about an extraordinary little book called *The Power of the Powerless*. The author, Christopher de Vink, recounted how Oliver, his brother, had been born blind. He couldn't see, and he couldn't speak. He couldn't even lift his head. He had to be spoon-fed and sponge-bathed. Every day, someone had to change his diapers. And his condition never changed.

Oliver lived down the hallway in his brother's home. Over the years, many walked down that hallway. Some stayed to visit. Others who met Oliver never took off their coats and said they had to leave, as did Christopher's first girlfriend.

I said to Don, "One thing held true for all: Anyone who saw Oliver had to look at himself. Reading Oliver's story was like standing in the doorway of his room. It made me wonder, would I have found a convenient reason, like Christopher's girlfriend did, to be on my way? Or would I have seen in Oliver a person who, just like me, was born with a need for acceptance, friendship, and love?"

The de Vink family did. For thirty years they loved Oliver even though he was literally powerless to love them back. In caring daily for Oliver, they learned to live outside of their comfort zone. "What, at first, must have seemed frustrating and fruitless to Oliver's family," I said to Don, "eventually became, for them, a normal way of life."

For Don Mowat, "normal" meant returning to Eastern Europe and Bosnia with Molly for an extended visit. While we stayed in touch I began to think out loud with groups who invited me to tell my story. In the summer of 1997, I had an opportunity to give the short program at the Seattle "4" Rotary luncheon. Of the five or six hundred in attendance, I saw a few people I recognized.

But it was a total stranger in the audience who reached out his hand the next day and made me an offer I couldn't refuse.

Smart decision

The next day at a Seafair board meeting, Phil Smart Jr., the president of a Seattle Mercedes-Benz dealership, approached me. He and his father had heard me speak at the Rotary luncheon and wanted to know if I would be interested in giving a presentation to their dealership team. "I would love to," I said, already looking forward to getting better acquainted with him and his father, who had started the business.

Two weeks later, we met over breakfast. Phil Smart Sr. greeted me with a warm handshake and was a natural curiosity. He was interested in everything and was a terrific listener. But I wanted to hear his story. He had served with General Patton in Tunisia during World War II. We talked about flying for a few minutes. Then, I asked him about his life.

Born and raised in Seattle.

Graduated from the city's Roosevelt High School, class of '37.

Married for fifty-plus years. Two children.

He had been a Boy Scout leader for as long as he could remember. Then, back in the late 1960s, a woman walked into his dealership. She hadn't come to buy a car but to sell Christmas cards to support the Children's Hospital and Medical Center.

Phil couldn't say no. During her visit, the woman, Peg Emory, learned that Phil had "retired" from his many years of volunteer service with the Boy Scouts. A few days later she called back with another offer.

"Phil, the chairman of the board at the hospital wants me to make you an invitation you can't refuse."

"What's that?"

"Since the hospital began in 1907, there's never been a male volunteer on any of the children's wards. We would like you to come to the hospital one night a week for three hours."

"That's all?" Phil said.

"Yes, three hours. Will you do it?"

That's how Phil started volunteering at The Miracle House. It's where he said he went to school. His tuition was zero. His subjects were fear, hope, life, death, vision, affirmation, determination, forgiveness, all subjects taught to him by teachers.

And his teachers were children. Many of them were quadriplegics who had been injured in car wrecks. Some had been paralyzed by shooting accidents or born with debilitating illnesses.

Phil confessed that every Christmas morning for the past twenty-four years, he has walked down the hall of wing 2-D dressed in a bright red suit and a long, flowing, synthetic white beard. "I have to go. After all, the children have written letters." He read me a few excerpts:

"Dear Santa, I would like to get out of this hospital."
"Dear Santa, I would like a Sega."
"Dear Santa, I would like a house for me and my mom. And some help with getting over my aggression. P.S.: I believe in you."

He told me another story.

One of my teachers was a little boy named Bobby. When I met him he had tubes running every which way and had been in the hospital most of his life. One day as I turned to step into his room, he said, "Here comes that angel from heaven, a car dealer!"

On Christmas morning, I found him talking on the telephone. He saw me and said, "Here comes the real Santa Claus, Grandpa. Want to talk to him?" He handed me the phone.

"Hello, Gramps," I said.

"Is this the real Santa Claus?"

"Yes, it is."

"How do I know?"

"Scout's honor," I said.

"How's my grandson?"

"He's doing marvelously well."

"Looks pretty good?"

"Sure."

"Gramps, where are you calling from?"

"I'm calling from Aberdeen."

Phil reminded me that the city of Aberdeen was about three hours by car from Seattle. He wondered why the boy's grandpa hadn't made the drive.

"I just checked the weather for the state. There's no snow forecast. Aberdeen isn't that far away."

"You don't understand," said the elderly man. "I'm calling from Aberdeen. Aberdeen, Scotland."

After the phone call with his grandpa, Bobby looked up at me and said, "Santa, what do you do with pain?"

"Well, because of my crooked fingers, Santa can't even point straight to the North Pole, so I have to take Advil. What do you do with pain?"

Bobby said, "I take pain and put it in a box and wrap it with tissue paper and bright ribbon and throw it away."

"Why?"

"I can't show pain," replied Bobby.

"Why not?" I asked.

"It hurts my mother's heart."

Phil dried his eyes, stared out the window, and said, "The next time I wrap a Christmas gift, I'll think about Dr. Robert Bayne, age ten. This morning he lies in a church cemetery in Aberdeen,

Scotland. He's my teacher who taught me about how short life is."

The amazing thing, besides his willingness to be touched by children, is what Phil learned by investing three hours a week. He found the time in what he called his "third eight."

"We've all been given the same amount of time: eight hours for sleep, eight hours for work, and eight hours to spend as we see fit. When I speak to audiences I ask them, 'What might happen in our world if you, if I, took a piece of that third eight and invested it in serving the hurting, the homeless, the unemployed, the young, the old, the illiterate, or the drugged? What would happen if we used our God-given talents, our energy, our courage, and our empathy? What would happen in Seattle, or Los Angeles, or wherever? I believe the world would change.'"

I looked at Phil and realized that in twenty years I would be his age. As I eavesdropped on a life of compassion, it was clear that I didn't have to spend a penny or go to school to make a difference in the lives of others. As Phil had already taught me that morning, I simply needed to be in the presence of great teachers who could continue to teach me how to love God and love others by how they lived their lives.

On an early Wednesday morning a month later, I walked into his showroom to speak. I couldn't avoid admiring the beautiful automobiles, or the owner. Phil Sr. and I have become good friends. He calls me Commander. I should call him blessed.

Within the span of three months I had met two distinctly different men, an entrepreneur and a luxury car dealer, whose journeys had led them to strikingly similar conclusions about the things that really mattered. Both had chosen to be vulnerable—with their emotions, and their time. They had chosen to love others, not because of what they could get in return, but because of what they felt privileged to give away to someone else. In Don Mowat and Phil Smart, I saw how Jesus would love people if He were eating with the homeless in Bosnia or walking down the hallway of a hospital in Seattle. The same kind of love could be a regular occurrence in my own life.

Sonya was modeling it for me in her spare time. She had been overwhelmed with the caring and comfort that hospice had provided to her mom in her struggle with cancer. Six months later she was a trained volunteer at the Evergreen Hospice live-in facility in Kirkland. Some people who learned what Sonya was doing said, "I couldn't do that." Sonya would tell them that caring for someone about to die is one of the most rewarding and fulfilling things she's ever done.

We spent Thanksgiving at the hospice center. I sat in the living area and observed Sonya and other volunteers as they quietly moved from room to room helping with the needs of people who wouldn't live until Christmas. I marveled at how attentive and responsive she was in offering her love. And when we left late that afternoon to spend the rest of the evening with friends, we both agreed that there couldn't have been a better way to spend the day.

I wanted to make compassion an integral part of my life. Even the days I blew it, I believed that if my life was going to be complete, I needed to be obedient. I recalled something Henri Nouwen had said in his book *The Inner Voice of Love*. "Sometimes little things build up and make you lose ground for a moment. . . . When all these come together, they can make you feel as if you are right back where you started. But try to think about it instead as being pulled off the road for a while. When you return to the road, you return to the place where you left it, not to where you started."[1]

When frustrations buffeted me and pulled me off the road, I thought of the people I was meeting who had helped awaken my mind and heart. If guys like Dave Dornsife, Don Mowat, and Phil Smart demonstrated Christ's love in its humblest form, then

Dave Baker brought home the fact that the decision to care for another could literally save one's life.

"At least I can be a dad…"

Dave Baker had spoken at our annual Good Friday leadership prayer breakfast I had organized in the San Francisco Bay area's San Ramon Valley. He was a big man, somewhere close to six feet nine inches tall and within shouting distance of four hundred pounds. After one of his patented greetings, I concluded that if you haven't been hugged by Dave Baker, you haven't been hugged. Gregarious and bright, he had been an All-American basketball player at the University of California at Irvine and had graduated at the top of his class at Pepperdine University Law School.

His success was instinctive and constant. He was elected to the Irvine city council, then became mayor. At the time, Irvine was the fastest-growing area and the biggest master-planned community in the country, and Dave was its rising star. He had become a visible force in the region's economic growth, when friends encouraged him to run for a seat in the United States Congress. Dave, a longtime republican, took the plunge and found himself in a neck-and-neck race. Two days before the election, his opponent distributed an anonymous direct-mail piece that shattered the calm of every mailbox. The headline said, "If Dave Baker's wife can't trust him, why should you?" (Dave had been open about difficulties much earlier in their relationship, and his wife was solidly behind him.) But this was politics, and votes, not truth, won elections.

With his campaign war chest out of money and his political future running out of time, Dave and his advisors decided to fire back with an eleventh-hour print piece. To pay for it, Dave wrote a check on a bank account of a major foundation on whose board he served, thinking he could cover the check with some personal funds due him from the proceeds of a real estate loan on their house that was closing the next day.

Having deposited the check, Dave told his wife his plans. While she supported him because she was also engaged in the battle, his explanation to her became a moral wake-up call. Forty-five minutes after cashing the check, he called the bank to cancel the check. In his mind it was "no harm, no foul." Dave, then, disclosed to his foundation board what he had done. But word of his hasty check writing leaked to the media, and within several months, he was suspended by the California Bar and out of a job.

Hounded by the press and struggling to pay his bills, Dave returned home from another difficult day of trying to stay ahead of the wolves. When he got in the door, his wife said, "Dave, you've been a professional grenade catcher. I'm tired of getting hit with shrapnel every day." His marriage was over.

Dave Baker had reached the end. His prayers to God seemed unanswered. Desperate for answers and feeling only the darkness, he decided to end his life. Late that night, he contemplated how he would ram his Mercedes-Benz into a cement pillar. His only question was should he say good-bye to his four-year-old son, Sammy, and his seven-year-old son, Ben, still asleep upstairs.

At that moment, Sammy came downstairs wearing his pajamas. He stopped and paused inches away from Dave and then wiped the tears from his dad's eyes. Then Sammy turned and left just as quietly to go upstairs. As dawn rose, Dave neared the door to the garage. He then heard a noise at the top of the stairs. He looked up and saw Sammy, who had come to get a ball.

"Here, Dad, just play catch with me."

Dave Baker stopped. The light from the upstairs window framed his son's angelic profile as Dave froze in place, his heart and his mind a swirl of emotions and thoughts. Suddenly a thought broke free from the abyss, and Dave realized, "There may not be anything left in my life, but I am still Sammy Baker's dad."

To be so close to dying—and so grateful for living. . . .

Dave's story made me think of another man who made a different choice. In 1996, the body of Admiral Mike Boorda, the Chief of Naval Operations, was found near the Navy Memorial in Washington, D.C., with a fatal gunshot wound to the chest. A shocked Navy and American public asked, "Why would such a distinguished military leader take his own life?" He assumed his position in the wake of the Navy's Tailhook scandal, and the Navy was receiving adverse publicity on a number of fronts. On the eve of a *Newsweek* magazine disclosure about the Admiral's unauthorized wearing of the "Combat V" award on his Vietnam Campaign medals, he brought the ultimate judgment against himself.

Admiral Boorda picked up a gun and met death. Dave Baker picked up a ball and found life. By finding God when it mattered most, he literally looked up and saw his future because of his courage to connect in the heart of another.

For Dave Dornsife, it was a nomad.

For Don Mowat, it was a refugee.

For Phil Smart, it was a child.

And for Jim Horsley, it was friends. Friends who showed him their hearts.

11

Learning to Dance

Courage is the price that Life exacts for granting peace,
The soul that knows it not, knows no release
From little things;
Knows not the livid loneliness of fear,
Nor mountain heights where bitter joy can hear
The sound of wings.

—AMELIA EARHART[1]

The crowd of barefoot African children and adults stared at the
miracle in my hand. Soft murmurs erupted in shouts. In less
than sixty seconds, the soft, brown face of a boy had emerged
into a Polaroid photograph. Kids crowded in, adults smiled in
awe, and then a small forest of hands filled the air. I checked the
film counter; I had nine more miracles to use up.

I was back in Senegal, this time with some donors who wanted
to see how water was changing life in the villages where World
Vision wells had been dug. But before seeing the projects, I
wanted them to experience what a village without a well looked
like, and how the people lived. Women had to arrive at the hand-
dug well at dawn in the hopes that enough water for their
children had seeped in overnight. Children were diseased and

covered with sores. The heat was stifling, and the wind drove the sand into every pore. This particular village was on the list to get a well in the near future. For now, life remained miserable.

I knelt down until I was at eye-level of the children. I couldn't take the picture; a frowning village elder kept trying to jump in the picture. I tried not to seem distracted, but the man wouldn't stop. I thought maybe he didn't want me taking pictures, but our project manager assured me that we were okay to continue. I briefly turned to one of the donors and said, "I wonder what it would take for that guy to smile."

I didn't think anything about my comment, until a few minutes later. With the photo session over, I walked over to a small group of villagers, and noticed the dour looking man standing next to his hut. At his side, a young boy was doubled-up and leaning on a long stick. I asked the World Vision field director about the boy, and she told me that he had been crippled by polio. The man's other son was lying on the dirt floor inside the hut. He, too, had polio and was so crippled he couldn't walk.

I looked at them and said nothing. The next morning, I got up earlier than usual for some private time before our day got under way. As I reflected on the man I'd seen the previous afternoon, I began to weep. Not because I felt like I could have fixed his situation, but because I had missed the moment. I had missed the chance to reach out and connect in the life a father who loved his kids as much as I loved mine. He was so worthy of attention, and I had been so flip. Not intentionally, but just the same, I had failed to grasp the opportunity to at least offer some caring to the man who was in such pain over the suffering of his boys. Sitting on the edge of the bed in my hotel room, I vowed that I would not miss another opportunity to care for a person God might put in my path. I just never expected to find it only a few miles from my home.

Where I needed to be

I had just finished speaking at a Rotary Club in Seattle where I concluded my talk with a challenge. "Find a way," I said, "to model the courage and hope that's alive in someone like Don Mowat, or Phil Smart, and connect in the life of another person. With Christmas fast approaching, find a way to touch the life of someone in need."

Afterward, as the crowd milled around, a tall gentleman reached out and handed me a business card. On the back he had scribbled, "Steve, Harrison House." *

"This guy," he said, pointing to the name he had scribbled on the back of the card, "is a Vietnam veteran. He's dying from a cancerous brain tumor. I think he'd appreciate a visit from you."

"I'll take a look at it," I replied. What I didn't say is, "Where on earth am I going to find the time for this?" Then I remembered the words I'd spoken just minutes before. That night, after tracking down a phone number, I called Harrison House, which happened to be a hospice-type facility in the area.

"A friend suggested I come by to see Steve," I told the receptionist. "What arrangements do I need to make to visit him?" All I had to do was come by.

The next morning I phoned Bill, who had handed me the card at Rotary. "How sick is your friend?" I asked. He said no one had expected Steve to live long enough to celebrate his forty-ninth birthday, three weeks earlier.

"How much time do you think he has?" I asked.

"We didn't think he'd live to his forty-ninth birthday or to Thanksgiving, but he's still with us. But he could die this afternoon," said Bill.

After figuring out how to rendezvous with Bill, I looked at my watch. It was a forty-five-minute drive to Bothell. I cleared my

* Names changed out of respect.

197

schedule for the next two hours, walked outside, and jumped in my pickup truck. I wasn't going to sit this one out.

Harrison House was an attractive four-bedroom, single-story home in a quiet, residential neighborhood. In a comfortable, nicely appointed bedroom that included a fireplace and a pleasant view, I met Steve. He lay asleep in his hospital bed. His head was swollen, and his mottled face was puffy. Balding and clean-shaven, he looked completely different than the picture on the nightstand of him with his girlfriend.

Bill reached over and touched Steve's shoulder.

"Steve. . . . Steve, wake up. I want you to meet Jim Horsley, a friend from Rotary. He's a Vietnam vet. He's also flown with the Blue Angels." I knew Bill was just trying to build a bridge.

While his introduction hung in the air, I could hear the words of Henri Nouwen I had read recently about his work in a home near Toronto for the developmentally disabled. "These broken, wounded, and completely unpretentious people forced me to let go of my relevant self—the self that can do things, show things, prove things, build things—and forced me to reclaim that unadorned self in which I am completely vulnerable, open to receive and give love regardless of any accomplishments."[2]

I knew, instantly, that if I was going to relate to Steve, it was going to be on his terms, not on the basis of my resumé. After a few minutes Bill left, and I began to learn a little about the man I had come to see. Steve had completed two tours of duty in Vietnam. Serving in the army, he had been stationed north of Saigon in the central highlands and had come home with two Purple Hearts. For a number of years he had worked in an auto dealership's paint and refinishing department, and he loved to remodel antique cars.

About six months earlier, he had fainted twice within a week and had gone to see a doctor. Lab tests revealed his worst nightmare: He had an inoperable brain tumor. I learned a few other things. He had been married and divorced four times. His only son was now in prison.

Though we had little in common, we had both served in combat. The shared experience of war made us feel a little less like strangers. While he said very little, I didn't rush in to fill the silence.

"I just wanted to spend some time with you," I said. We talked for fifteen minutes or so, and he told me that he wasn't in any pain and that a lot of his swelling was due to the steroids that were being prescribed for him. He soon started to tire, and I asked him, "Would you mind if I pray for you before I leave?"

"Not at all," he said.

I took his hand. It was ice cold, but he gripped my hand firmly. I prayed for Steve's comfort and that he could experience God's peace and presence in this very difficult time.

As I got ready to leave, I said, "Steve, I'll see you in a few days."

On my way out, I met his girlfriend. "I had to bring him here," she said. "I couldn't care for him on my own anymore." While admitting she felt a little guilty about having to move Steve into the home, she still felt she had done the right thing.

A few days later I came back. Steve had told me he liked candy, so I brought a box of chocolates, which he eagerly began to devour. Two days before Christmas I brought a box of Mrs. Field's cookies. I told him a little bit about myself, including the long, slow journey of coming home to a God who loved me in all my broken places. I didn't know if he would understand or not.

"Do you remember how good it felt coming off the front lines in Vietnam?" I said. "Remember what it felt like to sleep in clean sheets, take a hot shower, and eat a warm meal? That's what God offers us. He takes us out of the war and gives us a place of peace."

Steve didn't say much. I didn't see or hear any evidence of God in his life. There was no sense of eternity or what it might take to get there. Yet, I didn't feel like I had to "fix" Steve's spiritual condition. That was God's work, not mine.

The next visit a few days later, I asked him, "Did my conversation last time make you nervous?"

"No."

"Did you spend any time thinking about anything I said?"

"Not really." And as I had done on my previous four visits, I prayed for Steve while holding his hand.

I was beginning to see signs that Steve's health was deteriorating. During my first visit, I had watched him consume a tuna melt, a whole box of cheese crackers, and a bowl of candy, all within ten minutes. The next week he was having trouble eating a piece of crust, and a few days later, a nurse was feeding him lunch with a fork. A few days later I came by, and he could barely lift a cup of water to his mouth and hardly had enough strength to talk. I doubted I would see Steve again, because I was heading into a hectic three-week travel schedule that included yet another trip to West Africa. Before I left, I ended our time with a simple prayer. His breathing had become heavy, and he appeared to be asleep. As I released my hand, he cracked open one eye and said, "Thanks."

I had never spent time in the presence of someone whose life was slipping away in front of me. Yet, when I met Steve, I learned something about myself. I could find a way to connect with a man whom, in any other circumstance, I might not ever have met. I didn't have any expectations that I was the bearer of miracles, or that Steve's life would be transformed by my presence. But I felt that Steve came to my attention in a way that was more than circumstantial. And I wasn't about to look past him when his need was put squarely in my path.

Hard-wired for relationships

I never wanted the Blue Angels to be the best thing I've ever done. And it isn't. Surely, those two brief years in the sky became my most visible public accomplishment. I know I'm one of a few pilots in the world who have flown five hundred miles per hour in precision formation, a sleeve-length apart from the shiny blue skin of another Navy A-4 Skyhawk. Unforgettable? Absolutely. The best? No way. I'm absolutely convinced that my best days are ahead.

It has occurred to me that my years in aviation provide an interesting parallel in the continuum of life, marriage, and faith. When I left college and headed for Navy flight school, everything was new, and learning each new skill was an exciting adventure. When I received my Wings of Gold after eighteen months of intensive flight training, I found that learning to fly the A-6 was relatively easy. It was such a well-designed aircraft that it didn't take much to figure out how to take off, execute some basic maneuvers, and land. However, learning how to employ the aircraft as an aircraft carrier-based attack weapons system platform was a three-year process. It took enormous study, practice, simulator time, and more combat experience than I would have preferred.

About the time I thought I had the aircraft, its mission, and the environment it operated in pretty well handled, the whole scenario changed. I had learned to attack stationary land-based targets in Vietnam. But when the war ended, because of the threat of the Soviet Navy we had to figure out how to attack a heavily-defended Soviet ship at sea. This was a completely different deal. As we retrofitted the A-6 with new computers and a laser tracking system, I had to regroup and learn a new weapons system modification.

That's kind of the way it's been for me in life and in relationships. I've had to continually learn to adapt to new situations and circumstances when it would have been more comfortable to stay with what I knew. The only difference is that when I flew, I didn't set myself on fire, which is essentially what I did in my personal life.

I don't know if I'm a whole lot different than a lot of men in my age group, but I did a lot more preparing for my aviation career than I ever did in my personal life. When Sonya and I married, I was twenty-two and she was twenty-one. We hadn't read a marriage book or been to a marriage class. It took me until I was thirty-seven years old to find a personal relationship with God and experience His presence. I was forty-two when I began dealing with my past and understanding, on a true emotional level, how my past could inform my future. I wasn't necessarily a slow learner, I just got started late. It's never too late, because the last ten years have been the best of my life.

Every day I focus not only on what I need to learn but also on what I do with what I know. Ignorance may be bliss, but not in marriage, life, or faith. It has taken a completely different kind of courage for me to live out some of the relational experiences I've talked about in this book than it did to get shoulder-to-shoulder with five other guys flying shiny blue jets.

It has taken the courage to confront how imperfect I really am as a work-in-progress. It has taken the courage to change not only my perspectives but also my willingness to lift the visor on my emotions and live life outside my comfort zone. It has taken the courage to risk rejection and sorrow to reach out and touch the life of another. I've shared stories with you of those who have done it better than I, but in helping another, there are no losers.

By choosing to live like they have—by connecting in the life of an individual—whether drinking warm camel's milk in the desert, or praying with a sick friend—I've discovered who God really intends me to be.

I've discovered that, like it or not, we're all hard-wired for relationships. And that begins with my relationship with the One who created me. I've found that if I'm not right with God, it doesn't work very well for me anywhere else. Living into this truth has not been easy. However, every so often in life, God provides a milepost that shows us how far we've come. For me, that marker was my daughter's wedding.

I was fine during the wedding rehearsal and dinner afterwards. Then came the next day's memory of a lifetime. The church was decorated, the crowd was standing, and the music started. I pushed open the doors to the chapel, and Shannon put her arm in mine. As we walked down the aisle, I discovered why they call it a wedding march. I reveled in the moment, while at the same time choking with emotion. This was my little girl, and she had grown into a woman.

The baby born on the day I bombed Hanoi's Gia Lam rail yard.

The petulant five year old who heard me say, "Don't spray that shaving cream on me," and then did it anyway.

She was the teenager who confronted the distortions that had clouded my sky.

And now she had become a beautiful young woman, headed to the altar to begin her future with Gary. The moment could not have been better, and I could not have been prouder.

As we gathered together for the traditional pictures, I was overcome with the blessing that my family has been in my life.

Jeff, who offers kindness and understanding and is such a good listener.

Shannon, who has taught me perspective and sensitivity, and never gives up.

And Sonya, who has shown such tenderness and patience, such support and encouragement. Each of them and all of them have given more forgiveness, love, and joy to me than I could have ever hoped for.

After giving a speech, people will often come up to me and ask, "How did you get to where you are?" I've seen it in their eyes. They think the grass is greener on my side, when in reality they don't know I'm still pulling weeds. What they're really asking are the questions I've often tried to hurdle without tripping:

"How much time will it take?"

Answer: a lifetime commitment. There will never be enough time to do everything we want, but there's more than enough time to do what is important. Don't take my word for it. Ask Phil Smart Sr.

"How much will it cost?"

When I went to work for World Vision, I lopped my income in half. Our family went from a spacious half-million-dollar home on a golf course to a three-bedroom rental that made the Leaning Tower of Pisa stand tall. We found out we could live just fine without club memberships, expensive cars, and big homes. Sonya has made every house a home, and we still dressed nicely and never missed a meal.

One of the principles I discovered during life's transitions is that it's impossible to reach for something better with two hands when I'm hanging on to what I have with one. There is risk, and there is a cost. That is the way it should be, because without both, it's probably not worth pursuing in the first place.

"What's the pay-off?"

Of the three questions, this is the easiest one for me to answer. I don't even have to ask people like Don Mowat, Phil Smart, or Dave Dornsife to add up the value of their life choices. It's written in their smiles. And I can't begin to measure the ultimate reward that comes from seeing the thanks in a mother's eyes when you've had an opportunity to help her child. I believe completely in God through Christ who undergirds it all, and I'm willing to bet my life on it. I wouldn't want to be in a position to have Jesus ask me, "Jim, why should I be in relationship with you for eternity when you wouldn't make room for Me on earth?"

It's not what we have that matters....

While I don't claim to have arrived, I've discovered that finding the courage to confront the reality of my own humanity, the courage to change what is needed, and the courage to care for others outside my comfort zone has led me into a different kind of life. It's a life that has little to do with arriving at personal success and has everything to do with discovering the ultimate in significance this side of heaven.

On the day I spoke at the Seattle "4" Rotary, Don Mowat introduced me to a woman named Shirley Lansing. Though she had sterling business credentials, she also had a story to tell. That afternoon, and later as we visited in her office, she told me what so many in our area already knew.

Her son, Jack, a U.S. Army helicopter pilot, was sent to the Persian Gulf to serve in Operation Desert Storm. On February 27, the day before the ceasefire, he was waiting to be airlifted out of Iraq to Kuwait. Jack decided to take the second of the two last helicopters to Kuwait. Once airborne, the pilot of the Blackhawk, perhaps confused by the smoke of burning oil fields in the region, flew into Iraqi airspace over a heavily fortified Republican Guard airfield. The helicopter was shot down, sending soldiers, including Shirley's son, to their deaths.

In March 1991, while the tragedy was still fresh in her mind, Shirley stood on the platform at a Billy Graham Crusade in Seattle and looked out on an audience of fifty-three thousand people who filled the Kingdome that Sunday afternoon.

"Jack committed his life to Jesus when he was young," she said. "At the time it didn't seem terribly important, but it was. . . .

"Three weeks before he was killed, Jack sent two letters home, to be opened 'just in case.' After we got the news, we opened our letter, and it said, 'Well, if you have to open this, please don't worry about me. I'm all right, and for once, I know something you don't—what heaven's like.'"

Later that afternoon, thousands in the audience stood in front of the platform as a literal and symbolic demonstration of their new or renewed faith in Jesus Christ. A woman who had volunteered as a counselor later contacted Shirley and told her of two conversations she had at the Crusade. One had been with a woman who said, "I came to this event feeling bitter because I lost a son in Vietnam. I've not been willing to forgive God for taking my son, until now. If Shirley Lansing could lose a son and find peace with God, I thought, so could I."

The second conversation the counselor related to Shirley had been with an elderly lady. "When that woman told the story of her son, I believe God was showing me the way to heaven. And I'm ready to meet Him there."

By finding the courage to talk about her son's death, Shirley Lansing showed me a great and often overlooked truth, that it's not what we have that counts, but it's what we do with what we have. What would always be a poignant memory for her had now become a life-changing opportunity for others to begin a personal, eternal relationship with God.

A true story of hope

I've yet to find words to describe what the people in this book have found. The closest I came to getting my arms around it was when I gave Tad the pictures of his dad, or when, as a young father, I saw Jeff or Shannon smiling at me as they stood up in their cribs and reached their arms out to me.

I know it has to do with love. Joy comes close to defining it, this sense of completeness everyone's seeking in life though few have found. T. S. Eliot may have captured it when he wrote:

We shall not cease from exploration
And the end of all our exploring

Will be to arrive where we started
And know the place for the first time.[3]

If I could take along one story during the rest of my life's journey, it would have to be one of hope. It would begin with the picture of a Romanian orphan, a young, physically handicapped little girl whose face filled up the television screen from a World Vision video. She was one of thousands of orphans who had survived inside the cages during the horrific reign of Nicolae Ceausescu. His long-overdue demise opened the door for relief organizations like World Vision to help thousands of children live again.

And one of them was this tiny, little girl whose straight brown hair framed a pair of twinkling eyes and an infectious grin. In my fundraising efforts to secure help for these children, I saw a photograph of the same little girl in a World Vision newsletter. She had been adopted by a woman named Heidi Fortcamp and her husband, Monti, who lived north of San Francisco in the city of Santa Rosa.

In the course of a single phone call, I learned the story of how Heidi had gone to Romania on her own because she wanted to make a difference in the life of one small child she hoped to bring home. Heidi thought her prayers had been answered when she saw a little brown-haired girl.

Her name was Petronella. She had lived in the overcrowded squalor of a nursery filled with 150 children that had one bathroom and only two staff workers. In the dead of winter, the building had little warmth, and the children had little to eat.

Petronella had two severely deformed arms. She barely had fingers, and she had been severely traumatized. After failing to convince the Romanian authorities that she could offer Petronella a home in the United States, Heidi flew home. Weeks later she returned, determined to convince Romanian officials that she could help Petronella. The officials finally agreed to let her bring Petronella home, with the stipulation that any adoption would be contingent on Heidi returning to Romania with Petronella after the American doctors had completed their examinations and recommendations for corrective surgery.

When I saw Petronella the first time, she was banging on pots and pans she had scattered on the floor of Heidi's kitchen. With her two fingers she could hold a spoon and was feeding herself. I couldn't believe it was the same child I had seen in the dimly lit video. I was captivated. Though she hadn't learned to speak, I knew her mom could tell the story.

"Would you be willing," I asked Heidi, "to share what's happened with our church congregation during a worship service?"

"I would be honored," she said.

Before an attentive Sunday morning congregation, I interviewed Heidi. She talked about her initial interest, about seeing this little girl for the first time and wanting to take her home. She talked about bringing her home to Santa Rosa, about the anticipated operations on her back and hands. She talked about giving Petronella a new name. They called her Hope because of what they wanted to offer in her future and what they could share together. And Hope was as precocious as any four-year-old I'd ever seen. She squirmed and giggled, and waved at the audience. Heidi began to cry.

"We know we've agreed to take her back to Romania. We have no guarantee the officials will let her come back home and live with us. But by God's grace we're trusting that this is going to turn out the right way.

"For now we're willing to take the risk. Even if we had to say good-bye, Monti and I would rather have had the time she's been with us than to not have had any time with her at all. Whatever pain we might have to deal with later has been worth the joy we've already experienced."

Hope's story is still being written. Her life changed forever when two people found the courage to step beyond their comfort zone to love her, totally and unconditionally.

Heidi and Monti may not take the ultimate credit for her life, but they are living out the meaning of this little girl's name. Croatian Pastor Peter Kuzmic said it best:

Hope is the ability to hear the music of the future;
faith is having the courage to dance to it today.

The thundering roar of Blue Angel air shows has been replaced by a much sweeter refrain in my life. By any measure, I haven't arrived, but God has certainly brought me to place of hope that is far better than I would ever have found on my own. While He has provided the music for my future, and while I'm still learning the steps, I can take comfort in knowing that I'm surrounded by a family and friends who love me, that I'm headed in the right direction, and that I've been gifted to do the things He has set before me.

The apostle Paul wrote, "Not that I have already obtained all this, or have already been made perfect. . . . But one thing I do: Forgetting what is behind and straining toward what is ahead, I press on toward the goal to win the prize for which God has called me heavenward in Christ Jesus" (Philippians 3:12–13).

And that prize is available to all of us. By living a different kind of courage.

One Final Word...

Since the time I finished writing this book, a few lives have changed.

Tad Clark completed his flight training with the United States Air Force. He's been assigned as a T-37 jet fighter instructor at Sheppard Air Force Base in Wichita Falls, Texas.

Dave Dornsife and I have traveled (once again) to West Africa.

Sonya continues to expand her care-giving role for the elderly who are alone and sick. Our most recent best day together was kayaking on Seattle's Lake Union, followed by a romantic luncheon at a nearby waterfront restaurant.

Hopefully, the best of my story is still being written. And so is yours.

Today, I'm facilitating seminars and workshops for business professionals who are seeking more intentionality in their quest for a life of significance and their desire to answer the question "What's next?"

If you or your organization would like to know more about these opportunities, particularly the issues and ideas in this book, please contact me. I would enjoy hearing from you.

26137 104th Ave. S.E., Suite 173
Kent, WA 98031
Phone: 206-890-3008
Fax: 206-417-9874
E-Mail: Jim@jimhorsley.com
Web site: jimhorsley.com

JIM HORSLEY

Notes

Chapter 1

1 Samuel Fessenden, Speech, June 1896, Republican National Convention, St. Louis, Mo.

Chapter 2

1 Antoine de Saint-Exupéry, *Wind, Sand, and Stars* (New York: Harcourt Brace, 1967), 63.

Chapter 3

1 Henry Kissinger, *The White House Years* (Boston: Little Brown, 1979), 230.

Chapter 4

1 Roy "Butch" Voris, Captain, U.S. Navy (Ret.), *Blue Angels* (Pensecola, Fla.:United States Navy).

Chapter 5

1 Brucc Davey, Lieutenant Commander, U.S. Navy, 1980.

Chapter 7

1 Michael Norman, *These Good Men* (New York: Crown Publishers, 1989), 293.

Chapter 8

1 Simone Weil, *First and Last Notebooks*, ed. Richard Rees (New York: Oxford University Press, 1970), 77.
2 Henri J.M. Nouwen, *The Wounded Healer* (New York: Image Books, 1972), 88.

Chapter 9

1 Betty Edwards, *Drawing on the Right Side of the Brain* (New York: Putnam, 1989), 23.

Chapter 10

1 Henri J.M. Nouwen, *The Inner Voice of Love* (New York: Doubleday, 1996), 38.

Chapter 11

1 Mary S. Lovell, *The Sound of Wings* (New York: St. Martin's Press, 1989), iv.
2 Henri J.M. Lovell, *In the Name of Jesus* (New York: Crossroads Publishing, 1997), 16.
3 T.S. Eliot, *The Four Quartets* (San Diego: Harcourt Brace, 1971), 59.

About the Authors

JIM HORSLEY is active in public speaking, seminars, and retreats, partnering with organizations to achieve greater commitment and contribution to their vision and objectives. In addition to flying combat missions in North Vietnam as a jet aviator with the Navy, he spent a two year tour as a demonstration pilot with the Blue Angels. The father of two grown children, Jim and his wife Sonya live in the Seattle area.

MARK CUTSHALL is a full-time writer who specializes in helping individuals and organizations tell their stories. In addition to co-authoring seven books, he has written for numerous national magazines. Mark and his wife Linda live with their two children, Ryan and Sarah, in Seattle.